THE OLIVE GROVE

TRAVELS IN GREECE

><

KATHERINE KIZILOS

LONELY PLANET PUBLICATIONS
Melbourne • Oakland • London • Paris

The Olive Grove: Travels in Greece

Published by Lonely Planet Publications
    Head Office: 90 Maribyrnong St, Footscray, Vic 3011, Australia
                           Locked Bag 1, Footscray, Vic 3011, Australia
    Branches: 150 Linden St, Oakland, CA 94607, USA
                           10a Spring Place, London NW5 3BH, UK
                           1 rue Dahomey, 75011, Paris, France

Published 1997
Reprinted 2000

Printed by SNP Printing Pte Ltd, Singapore

Author photograph by Simon Bracken
Maps and design by Adam McCrow
Edited by Janet Austin

National Library of Australia Cataloguing in Publication Data

Kizilos, Katherine, 1960- .
The olive grove: travels in Greece

ISBN 0 86442 459 0.

1. Kizilos, Katherine, 1960- – Journeys – Greece.
2. Greece – Social life and customs – 20th century.
3. Greece – Description and travel.
I. Title. (Series: Lonely Planet journeys.)

949.5076

Text © Katherine Kizilos 1997
Maps © Lonely Planet 1997

LONELY PLANET and the Lonely Planet logo are trade marks of Lonely
Planet Publications Pty. Ltd.

Katherine Kizilos was born in Australia in 1960. She has lived in Greece and travelled throughout the country. Katherine now lives in Melbourne, where she works as a journalist.

For my family, near and far

ACKNOWLEDGMENTS

A great many people have helped me to write this book. I would especially like to thank John Burke and Linda Connolly for their interest, for the books they lent me, for reading the work-in-progress and for their suggestions; Angela Khoury for her conversation, her work on the transcripts and her encouragement; Dennis Pryor for his help on the islands section; and Karen Kissane for her moral support and good advice on editing the material.

I am grateful to the Greek Ministry of the Aegean and the Greek Press Ministry for their goodwill and practical assistance, with particular thanks to Angelos Augoustidis. Mark Mazower's book *Inside Hitler's Greece* was an invaluable source of information on the history of the German occupation of Greece during the Second World War. Also, thanks to all of those who shared their stories with me, giving no thought as to how it might profit them – without these tales I would have had no book to write. Some of the people I met on the road are named in the book, other names have been changed for reasons of privacy; I am particularly indebted to Murat Hattatoglu and Kosta Karagiourlis.

Special thanks to Vassili Kizilos for his companionship and generosity; to our neighbours in Chrysambela, particularly Antiopi and Pano Menzelopoulos, for their time and their courage; and to Apostoli and Katina Kizilos for helping us to make a second home in Greece. And finally, thanks to Sophia Kizilos for all the work she did to help me write this book, both in Greece and in Australia; to Angelo Kizilos for his stories, his translations and for his steady faith in the project; and to Tony and Dylan Lintermans for coming with me on the journey and for their love, patience and support – driving, editing, listening and wishing me well – all along the way.

CONTENTS

Time Line

3000-1100 BC	Cycladic and Minoan civilisations
1900-1100 BC	Mycenaean Age
1450 BC	Thira erupts
1200-800 BC	Dark Age
800-480 BC	Archaic (Middle) Age
480-338 BC	Classical Age
146 BC to 324 AD	Roman rule
324-1453	Byzantine era
330	Constantine dedicates the 'New Rome' of Constantinople, and the centre of the Roman empire moves from Rome to the Bosphorus
1204	crusaders sack Constantinople
1453-1829	Ottoman rule
1453	Ottoman Turks capture Constantinople
1821	Bishop Germanos raises the Greek flag at Patras, starting the Greek War of Independence
1829-present	Modern Greece
1829	Turks accept Greek independence
1912-13	the Balkan wars, which pitted Greece, Serbia and Bulgaria against the Ottoman Turks and ceded to Greece the Northern Aegean Islands and parts of Macedonia, Thrace and Epiros
1914-1918	First World War
1923	compulsory population exchange with Turkey agreed at the Treaty of Lausanne
1939-1945	Second World War
1946-49	Greek civil war
1967-74	military junta
1981	Andreas Papandreou becomes Greece's first socialist leader; Greece joins the European Community

I bent down to the vine,
its leaves shaking, to drink in
its honey and its flower;
and – my thoughts like heavy grapes,
bramble-thick my breath –
I could not, as I breathed,
choose among the scents,
but culled them all, and drank them
as one drinks joy or sorrow
suddenly sent by fate;
I drank them all . . .

from 'The First Rain' by Angelos Sikelianos

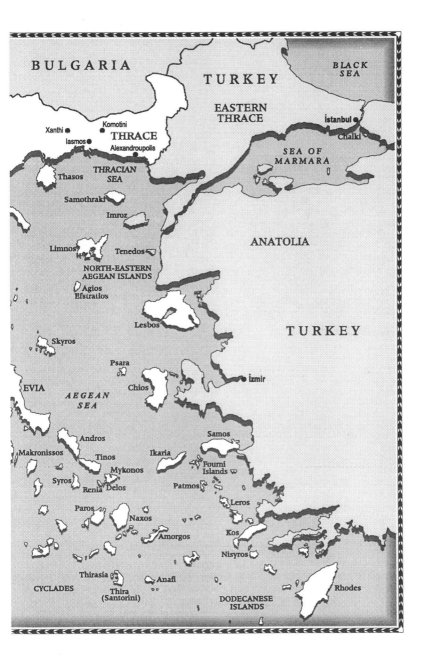

Beginnings

THE FIRST TIME I went to Athens I was seventeen. I had just finished my final high school exams, and was so excited to be travelling alone to Europe that I even enjoyed the twenty-hour plane journey from Melbourne. I had left without anticipating the pleasures of walking around a blue and white country. I did not know that, even in Athens, the colours of Greece are different, that the mountains are made of white rock and the buildings are marble and white cement and a shining blue sky spans it all. I did not know that the country, magically, was the colour of its flag. I knew nothing.

And I think now that this blend of excitement and blank ignorance is the perfect way to set out on a journey. Having no expectations, we make no judgments. This state of mind can augur well for travellers: it liberates us. We are free to greet each new sensation with a kind of wonder.

But then again, not all journeys are holidays.

><

My father, Angelo, paid my fare to Greece. He had migrated to Australia when he was not yet seventeen. He, too, had flown across the world alone, the most alone he had ever been – or ever would be, although he didn't know that then. He had not finished high school, even though he had been a good and diligent student, a lover of literature and history. He had savoured the stories he'd learned at school. Stories of Greek wars, which, when told in a Greek classroom, are inevitably moral lessons too: the Peloponnesian War, a study of hubris and its consequences; the dark years of the Turkish occupation; and the valiant Greek War of Independence. Thrilling stories, and Angelo's instinct had been to stick to his books; but history, in the form of the Greek civil war, stopped all that. After years of slaughter and uncertainty – my father's high school years also coincided with the German occupation of Greece during the Second World War – he'd wanted to escape, to emigrate and to leave all suffering behind him. "He begged me to go," my grandfather said later.

Blank ignorance. My father's passport photo shows a thin, smooth-faced boy, as pretty as a girl. In 1948 the aeroplane journey to Sydney took five days, as the KLM craft did not fly at night. The overnight stops were Teheran, Karachi, Bangkok and Darwin – places of unimaginable strangeness to a boy whose whole world had been a mountain village, a country high school and the wild stretch of mountains and coast between them. Angelo barely registered the other peoples, the other worlds, that flashed by him. He crossed the globe. To what? To see what? He didn't know.

In Darwin, he began to comprehend the magnitude of his journey when the boy behind him confessed that never, never could he have travelled so far if his father had not already been in Australia to greet him. Angelo knew no-one in Australia, and this solitary fact filled his mind as the plane flew over the great Australian loneliness, the desert in the centre of the continent.

The eventual landing in Sydney hit my father harder than he had been prepared for. His sponsor, a practical, money-making Greek who repelled him on sight, took Angelo to the Ritz: a milk bar and cafe he owned in central Sydney, in Pitt Street. Angelo was planted before a sink and a pile of dirty glasses and set to work. The job was relentless. He washed dishes for a sixteen-hour shift, with rest breaks that were few and perfunctory. No-one asked him how he felt, or talked to him much at all. He had escaped a war, and in doing so had exiled himself from his childhood, his language and his homeland. It was unusual for migrants to fly to Australia in those days; the air fare had been a small ransom and one that his family could ill afford. There was no returning home.

It was little wonder, then, that my father made a kind of religion of Greece and of his memories of home, such as they were. Because that is what he remembered: the hearth, the homeland, the mountains of his village, the olive groves, the still waters of the Gulf of Corinth. A hallowed and beautiful place. And so it is, truly. But memory and imagination lie side by side. I cannot remember Angelo talking about the country he had fled, the land of poverty and war. Nor did he praise Australia for its prosperity and peace.

Australia remained a place of exile for my father: flat, without history, its people racist and ignorant. He was proud of being Greek and abhorred being called a wog. In 1948 the pubs closed at six o'clock and you could only buy olive oil in little glass bottles from the chemist, where it was sold as a tanning aid. Politically and culturally, Australia was still in the shadow of Britain, a country my father reviled because he believed it had betrayed the Greek Resistance and so had helped to engineer the Greek civil war, the cause of his exile and suffering. He also despised Australia's other wartime ally, the United States, because that great and powerful friend had sold napalm and bombers to the Greek royalists. In Australia the whole bloody mess was dead and obscure: no-one cared, no-one believed him, it didn't matter. He hated the place.

><

When I first arrived in Athens, on a December morning in 1977, all of that was in my baggage, but I was too preoccupied with my own adventure to care. It was a cold, clear dawn and I stood on the tarmac wondering if I could see the Parthenon from there. A platoon of relatives I had never met, including my father's sister Angela and my cousin Peter, greeted me. We piled into a taxi and headed for Angela's flat. My Greek was poor; I felt my family's kindness and goodwill, but I was shy and barely spoke at first. Athens was alarming, jammed with people and traffic. Vast lighting and furniture emporiums, topped with billboards advertising Coca-Cola in both Greek and English, gave way to dark garages, their mouths agape, spewing towers of tyres.

Angela's flat was in Zographou, in a hilly street named after Greece's charismatic prime minister from the time of the Balkan wars, Eleftherios Venizelos. Zographou is a respectable suburb, but to my untrained eyes all of Athens was a mess of functional cement buildings and narrow streets, stewing under a cloud of exhaust fumes: the infamous *nefos*.

"Why does the city look like this?" I asked Peter. "Has there been an earthquake?"

He looked bemused. "What do you mean?" I pointed to the cracked pavements, the piles of building rubble on the kerbs, the plastic bags overflowing with garbage that littered the vacant lots.

A resigned shrug. "No earthquake, this is what it's like."

I stayed only a month on that first trip to Greece. In Athens I lived in Angela's immaculate apartment (and that is an irony of the city: that the chaos of the streets is unrelated to the meticulous order of the private, indoor world) and was dutifully shown the Parthenon and the National Archaeological Museum by Peter, a university student on his Christmas break.

Winter is the best time to visit Athens. The frantic tourism of the summer has long ended and the Parthenon stands in a pool of quiet – part inspiration, part reproach to the city below. It took me many visits before I saw the building with any freshness, before I saw it as it was. What I noticed at first were the incongruities. One grey morning I spotted a retired Australian news anchorman – recognisable even without his tie – leading a group of visitors from home. Behind them, a busload of Japanese stood patiently in line, each wearing identical plastic raincoats, name tags and cameras. It was a comic scene: the tourists looked displaced, even bored, but still they came.

Peter looked on disapprovingly. "I never come to these

places," he said. "But these old stones . . . it's all the foreigners care about."

His own sacred site was the Athens Polytechnic, the series of neo-classical buildings next to the museum where, in November 1973, thousands of students had gathered to protest against the military dictatorship that for seven years had replaced democratic government in Greece. The protest had been spontaneous, emotional, inspirational. The students gathered to sing songs and to make speeches about freedom and revolution; they stayed on the grounds of the Polytechnic for three days. Athenians, moved by their courage, donated tins of food and prayed for their safety. The protest ended when the tanks rolled in.

I have seen documentary footage of what happened next. The students held their ground and were silent as a sole voice pleaded with the men in the tanks, men they could not see: "Brothers, do not fire at us, we are Greeks like you." But the soldiers fired anyway. Around thirty students died; the exact number of casualties has never been established. But their defeat was illusory: soon after, democracy was restored in Greece.

For Peter, this story was more compelling and a greater source of pride than any pile of stones. Mostly, he saw the stones as a burden. "That's all the foreigners want to see . . ." He lived in a city that was revered for what it had once been and despised for what it now was. Despised by foreigners, anyway. They were another burden: the tourists who gawped at the country without understanding it, and the Great Powers who praised the ancients for giving the world democracy and yet who had deemed modern Greeks incapable of governing themselves. Peter told me all this in his steady, passionate way as we walked along Panepistimiou – University Street – the great avenue that leads into the dusty circus of Omonia Square.

Peter couldn't stay in Athens long because he was needed in the village to help with the olive harvest. I went with him, to meet the grandparents I had never seen and to visit Peter's father, Apostoli, and his wife, Katina. They all lived together in the house where my father had been born, near the square in Chrysambela, a village 500 metres above the coast of the northern Peloponnese. I arrived on a snowy night, and entered a room full of unfamiliar people, huddled around a fire in an old stone house.

Grandmother Katerina spent our first evening kissing my hand, staring at me tearfully and stroking my cheek. She sat on a bed next to a wood stove in a small, low-ceilinged room, whose floor threatened to give way whenever you walked upon it. Grandfather Vassili was more austere; a thin, upright, dark-haired man, he sat sizing me up under hooded eyes. Apostoli, his eldest son, and the only one to have stayed in the village, also watched as Katina served up brimming plates of stewed rabbit and potatoes. The table was covered with a sheet of plastic, with two knives in the centre for the six of us. The conversation was mostly about the weather: how long would the snow last and would the cold be severe enough to damage the olives. The discussion was threaded with a commentary on my tentative encounter with the rabbit. Apostoli cut morsels from his own plate and plonked them onto mine ("Try it, it's good!") as my grandfather relieved me of a strip of fat ("I can see you don't eat it"). I felt compelled to finish the meal despite my lack of appetite. It didn't matter. I had arrived in a place where I knew I belonged, and found people I would always love.

I don't know why we connect. I was too young to know that it happens rarely, when it happens at all. The bond I was forming with Greece was a personal one, with idiosyncratic variations. I resist the idea, for instance, that I like Greece because I 'found my roots' there, or because it helped to clarify my feelings of multicultural confusion. The ability to love more than one culture without confusion is commonplace, though rarely remarked upon. My father, it is true, was dislocated, and suffered keenly; I was much luckier. Roots can grow in more than one place, and living between two cultures, contrary to the stereotype, does not have to be a purgatory. Besides, most children of migrants don't live 'between' two cultures but within them. It is like loving more than one person; most of us can manage it. You embrace what is good and, if the love is to endure, you try and tolerate the rest.

I was particularly drawn to the landscape, which was quite different from anything I had known. The views around Chrysambela are wide, dramatic, even operatic. The village looks over the Corinthian Gulf to the mountains of Roumeli that rise on the other side. From its steep, olive-covered hills you can see Mt Parnassus, snow-capped and majestic, floating above the water. In my mind, I came to call my father's home Wuthering Heights. It wasn't a literal connection – the village is nowhere near a moor – but Emily Bronte's novel, with all its brooding passion, its longing and intensity, was the closest match I knew to the mood that mountainous landscape stirred up in me. In my teenage imagination, the beauty of the novel and of the landscape both sprang from a source that was dark, dangerous, tender and wild.

I kept going back to Greece. Over the next decade I went back four times and lived there for two years. Most of my time was spent in either the village or Athens, but I travelled to the islands and around the mainland as much as I could.

My last trip – the one before the journey described in this book – had been in 1987. My husband, Tony, and I spent most of that year living in the house my father had bought in Chrysambela. Most of our neighbours in the village had spent their lives watching their school friends, their relatives and their own children leave for Athens or, more dramatically, the strange maw of *xenitya*, the melancholy Greek word for a foreign place. These people had said farewell so often that they no longer saw their home with any clarity; very few saw it as we did, as a place of beauty and peace. So they were touched that we chose to live with them for a time. They laughed and shook their heads when we said no, no, it was we who should be grateful to them for their welcome.

In January 1988, just before we were due to return to Australia, the neighbours and relatives who had befriended us came to our house to celebrate St Anthony's Day. In the country the saints' days cannot be mistaken; the village church bells are rung in the morning as a reminder and a liturgy is performed. Our neighbours knew that Tony, an Anglican, did not celebrate his name day, but they came all the same, to drink his health and also to say goodbye. The women came with seasonal treats: *pergamonto*, the golden rind of a bitter citrus preserved in sugar syrup, and *melamakarina*, the traditional winter cakes flavoured with honey and walnuts. We received the ritual blessings: to go to the good and to return with a son. But mostly our neighbours had come to tell us that our holiday was over: "It is time for you to go home and to be serious."

I thought I would be back within two years, but it took me eight. I had rolled my eyes at the injunction to be serious, but that is what I became. The demands of my job, and of a new baby, conspired to prevent me from returning to Greece. Somehow, carelessly and against my will, my days became regimented and wretchedly busy. I longed for the life I had left behind, but the longer I stayed away, the more unreal it seemed. A mild panic that something precious had been lost would seize me whenever I thought about Greece. I particularly worried that the village might have changed irrevocably, so that even if I did return, I would not be able to experience the way of life I had treasured.

My grandfather had died since I had left (Katerina had passed away in 1979, soon after my first visit), and it was difficult to imagine the place without him. Apostoli, who had inherited the bulk of his land, was now in his seventies. He had been the most vigorous of men, and it was painful to think of him as being old. And it was not only members of my family who were ageing and changing: the village itself was on the wane. Already, in 1987, most of the people who had remained in Chrysambela were receiving old-age pensions; finding manual labourers to help them gather their olives and grapes was a persistent problem, and some had talked of abandoning their fields.

This pattern was being repeated all over Greece. The village life that for centuries had been the country's defining feature was clearly under threat. I had a selfish and irrational reason for caring about this. My life in Australia may have been out of balance, but somehow it made me feel better about the world if I knew that some harmony still existed in Greece. In my experience of the country, its best aspects flowed from the villages, and from the values instilled by village life (and some of its worst aspects too, it must be admitted). I wondered how the 'Greekness' that I loved would survive if the villages did not.

In the meantime my father had sold a cherry orchard that had been part of his inheritance in the village. He used to half-jokingly refer to this land as my dowry, and when he sold it he gave me half of the proceeds. That money made it possible for me to return to Greece. I planned a trip that would take me all over the country: to the islands, to the border lands of the north, and of course to the village as well.

As a child I had had little sympathy for my father's feelings of exile, for his insistence that happiness was not possible for him in Australia; I didn't like the fact that he relegated my birthplace – our home – to second best. But when I protested, all he heard was my lack of sympathy. For years my own feelings for Greece had run in tandem with this long-running battle with my father. My personal hope for the trip was that it would lead to a reconciliation of our differences; that we would somehow find a means to respect our separate understandings.

And so it was that in September 1995, loaded down with empty notebooks, a new camera and coffee-making equipment (to provide an alternative to the Nescafé that is consumed all over the country), I climbed aboard an Olympic Airways 747 and set off for Greece.

PART ONE

THE SEA

There still remains something for us to discover:
this light, these clusters of islands, what are they?
Are we dreaming?

from 'Draft for an Introduction to the Aegean World',
Odysseus Elytis

CHAPTER ONE

THE ISLAND OF WORK

T HE *NAIAS*, MY ferry to Syros, was big and crowded, as most inter-island ferries are during the season. It left Piraeus at 8 am, but even at that hour the port was hot, jostling with morning traffic, snarling maritime officials and overwhelmed tourists.

I envied the Greeks, most of whom had packed their clothes into a carelessly tied plastic bag. I, on the other hand, was forced to stagger, sweaty and muttering, under the weight of my suitcase; I cursed the dreadful stairs that blight the ferries of Greece (any staircase is dreadful once you have lugged a twenty-kilo case to the top of it). Recovering on the sundeck, I watched Piraeus retreat under the brown smear that stained the horizon. Goodbye *nefos*.

Relatively few foreigners bother with Syros. The *Naias* soon took on a garrulous holiday atmosphere that was distinctively Greek, as passengers lit cigarettes and settled cosily into gossip and idle chat. I eavesdropped on an account of a marriage: "He was unfaithful to her, that's true, but at least he never beat her . . ." Three middle-aged Greek women with crosses around their necks had fallen asleep on a bench. They reminded me of the three Fates of mythology, except that they had left their spindles and run away to sea. Their shoes were off, their feet had swollen in the heat; they slumbered peacefully, each with her mouth open.

On the water, the first islands loomed. Bony apparitions, these stark mountains of brown earth and white stone looked as unlikely and lovely as islands in a dream. Occasionally a road wound its way across a slope, like a mirage or a track in a desert. A road leading where? To service what? It was still morning but the sun was relentless; the only shade on those shores was thrown by rocks, or pooled in the creases of the mountains. I assumed the islands were uninhabited and dismissed the roads as some inexplicable folly, until I saw the silver flash of a car on one of them.

I leaned on the ferry rail and looked at the sea, the dazzle of it so much more beautiful than my creased and folded map of Greece, with its spore of tiny islands that I had dreamed and wished over during the months I had planned my journey. I willed myself to remember the excitement I had felt at the prospect of spending weeks sailing on the Aegean. My hand was trembling, and I had the fleeting sense that the happiness I had anticipated all winter long could suddenly evaporate into the blue. Then I spotted something I had never seen before: a school of dolphins leaping and splashing in the water ahead. Surely they were a good omen, I thought. Oh, let them be a good omen.

When Syros appeared, passengers gathered on the rails to look: the island was as brown and bare as the phantoms we had passed. Networks of dry-stone walls traced its contours, impressive and insane. What did they enclose? Piles of stones. I pointed them out to the middle-aged man who stood next to me.

"The walls are a beginning," he said.

"Of what?"

"Of housing. People are building here."

And yes, there *was* a house, an unadorned square of concrete, perched halfway up a rocky mountainside.

As the *Naias* continued its progress, these concrete outposts multiplied: villages of cement, surrounded by rubble. Eventually I realised that these brave dwellings were the suburbs of Ermoupolis, the famed neo-classical capital of Syros and of the Cyclades, the wonder I had come to see.

The ferry docked. Cranes leaned over the shipyard at one end of the harbour. In the noonday sun, Ermoupolis looked as functional and as pitiless as a factory.

In the port, I was a hostage to the heat; dragging my suitcase off the ferry took all my energy. A grey-haired lady bustled up, offering me a 'perfect' room and transport for my luggage. I toiled after her through the stony streets, having ceded my case to a man she had summoned.

The 'perfect' room was a small, stuffy triangle, but my benefactor believed that she could overcome my objections if she talked for long enough.

"My suitcase will barely fit in this room," I said. Nonsense, she replied, all that was required was a simple rearrangement of the furniture. To demonstrate, she deftly lifted a chair over our heads, out of the room and onto the street outside, placing it next to a table and a flowerbox of geraniums. "Now, isn't this just perfect?" My reply was interrupted by the roar of a passing motorbike; my landlady's smile became even more fixed and determined. Meanwhile, the man from the port had turned up with my suitcase, which he had somehow managed to heave to the pension; he remarked that the room was certainly "very beautiful." The man was no longer young, and my suitcase appeared to have taken its toll; he was sweating and looked unsteady on his feet. The sight of him convinced me that the room would do for a night.

><

Syros is one of the corners of a roughly equilateral triangle of islands in the centre of the Cyclades. The other two are Mykonos and Tinos, two islands which, in their own way, have links with the divine.

As everyone knows, Mykonos is a tourist phenomenon, a celebrated gay resort and nightclub nirvana. It is the closest island to Delos, the mythical birthplace of Apollo and Artemis. Delos, by all accounts, is small and barren. It puzzled the ancients, who wondered why the gods had been born in such an unpromising locale. Why was an oracle of Apollo located there? And yet the island has exerted tremendous power. The Cyclades are so called because the islands form a circle (cycle) around Delos. In modern times tourism has created another circle in the Aegean; the islands have been transformed by an ever-widening ring of ripples, starting with the big splash made by Delos/ Mykonos when international visitors began to flock there in the 1960s.

A French philologist, Jean Richer, believed he had solved the mystery of Delos. In the late 1950s he spent some time in Greece, where he was deeply affected by the atmosphere and siting of the sanctuaries of Apollo, particularly the home of his oracle at Delphi. Richer came to believe that the sacred sites of the ancient Greek world were determined by astrological alignments; sacred geography, as he understood it, was a system connecting the stars with the earth, the gods with man. He wrote that 'One rather gets the impression that the whole system of Greek islands was seen as the equivalent of the starry skies'.*

I don't know whether Richer was correct. His books received prizes from the Académie Française, but in his lifetime archaeologists resisted his findings. Yet his instinct that an esoteric science underpinned the ancient genius for the placement of temples is intriguing because the sites are still so powerful. Some magic remains. A sanctuary's purpose, its form and its setting combine to create a harmony, an overarching sense of rightness. The temple of Poseidon at Cape Sounion, near Athens, built to be seen against the sky and surrounded by the sea, is a good example of what I mean.

But it may be that Richer has unnecessarily complicated the matter. The secret of these sites may lie, more simply, in the aesthetic sensibilities of the people who built and used them. And how that developed, and why it has been lost, is a source both of wonder and regret. The historian Will Durant believed that Neolithic settlers built Europe's first civilisation on the islands of the Aegean, despite the practical difficulties, because they were enthralled by the islands' beauty; that the people who gave birth to our civilisation were inspired by their ecstatic plunge into the sea.

><

My room was at the working end of town, near the shipyard that dominates the port. In the late afternoon, I asked my landlady for directions to the square – all Greek towns have a square – hoping to find the centre of the city, but she was a shifty character, one of the most unreliable people I met during my stay on the islands. Her room was poorly situated, and this, combined with Syros's lack of tourist appeal, had convinced her that she could only survive by being *poniri*, or cunning, a folk attribute that is alternately a source of national pride and despair. All she would say was that her room was certainly very close to the bus stop and therefore in striking distance of all the island's beaches. Yes, but where was the square? A dour fruiterer was more helpful: "Just keep walking along this street and eventually you will find it."

The street was not promising. It was filled with earnest shops selling electrical appliances, lengths of pipe, drill bits. But as I approached the square the buildings became larger and more ornate, the shops livelier, and this built up a sense of expectation before the revelation of the square itself.

I once dreamt that my local shopping centre in inner Melbourne was transformed from a grimy jumble of disparately styled buildings into a peaceful piazza, where people sat to meet and talk. The Victorian town hall was no longer hidden by trucks, but bordered a flagstoned square. Hamburger joints and discount furniture shops had been replaced by restaurants and fountains. An ugly thoroughfare had been restored to its original architectural splendour; sanity and grace reigned.

My walk to the square in Ermoupolis recalled the dream, a rare instance of being able to track down one's sense of *déjà vu*. Miaouli Square was lined with neo-classical arcaded buildings, tavernas, bars and cafes. On one side was a massive town hall, built late last century by refugees from the Greek War of Independence, the conflict that finally ended Turkish rule. The effect was formal and grand; as I walked over the flagstones I imagined a fanfare of trumpets announcing my arrival. The square was full of people: talking, drinking or simply enjoying their evening promenade. At one end children were driving toy cars that were for hire, while their parents sat and drank coffee nearby. The atmosphere was neighbourly, even homely, so that the magnificence of the place felt incongruous and slightly comic, as though a local park led a double life as a grand opera set.

After the events of the day my expectations of Syros had been low, but with this change of scene I felt a surge of euphoria. I ordered ouzo and *mezedes* (or appetisers) at a cafe, where, for 500 drachmas, I could have tried what the English translation of the menu listed as 'fried nonsense'. To be in a Greek square on a summer evening was, in itself, a cause for celebration, and the setting matched my perception that now my journey had begun, and that the world was full of unexpected possibilities.

><

I soon found a new room, big, airy, cool and quiet, in a large neo-classical house that had seen better days. It was run by a little old lady and a little old man. I assumed that they were a married couple, but realised my mistake the following Sunday when I saw the little old lady go into the nearby Catholic church, while the little old man headed for the Greek Orthodox cathedral. The population of Syros is half Catholic, half Orthodox. The split defines the town: Ermoupolis is built on two hills, one for each denomination.

My room had a deep balcony that looked out over the street. On the corner was an *ouzeri* – a plain, well-scrubbed, old-fashioned place, with chairs and tables set out on the pavement. Every night an octopus was barbecued on a brazier just outside the entrance, where customers gathered and talked in soft voices. During the day the main customer was the plump electrician from the shop next door, who sat drinking coffee at a table, playing with his little dog and talking to his wife, whose habit it was to stand leaning against the door jamb.

The doings of the rest of the street were less visible. I was staying in the heart of the neo-classical district, and doctors, lawyers, architects and civil engineers had rooms in most of the buildings. Their discreet brass plates suited the city's architectural mood, but I wondered how an island of 22,000 people could possibly support all these professionals.

Directly below my pension was an old printer's office, which I discovered one hot afternoon when the still hours of the siesta were broken by a rhythmic clanking and whirring. The source of the noise was an old press cranking out a sheaf of advertising sheets. A rumpled, ink-stained man, a cigarette hanging from the corner of his mouth, saw me staring and called me into the shop for a closer look. "It's the only one left operating on Syros."

It was also, I realised later, a link to the island's historic publishing boom. Syros's first newspaper, the *Melissa*, appeared in 1830, heralding a new era of democracy and commerce in modern Greece, a country reborn after four centuries of Turkish occupation. Over the next seventy years, more than 160 newspapers were published on Syros, an output that was more than the island – or the nation – could possibly sustain. The boom was an expression of the energy and hope felt by the builders of Ermoupolis, before the bubble of their optimism burst and the publishers became redundant.

The printer's shop was narrow, cool and gloomy. It had been operating for 130 years and was now in a dishevelled, inky decline. Trays of letters and reversed metal images – maps, party logos – lay in the darkness. The floor was scattered with cigarette butts, and the arches in the wall were crammed with old newsprint, cardboard boxes and discarded ink pads. The presses no longer printed newspapers. A heavier, older English press with '1871' stamped on its side stood further back in the shop, and behind that was an even more primitive machine. 'Paris' (the only word on it that I could identify) was big enough to handle broadsheets and posters, and had a huge wheel so that at first sight it looked like a small cart. All the presses still worked, the printer told me with pride, although 'Paris' hadn't been touched in years.

"It's a museum," I said.

"Yes," he replied. "And in fact a museum wants this equipment, but we've decided to keep it for a while."

In the meantime, he was a self-appointed curator, presiding over an era's outmoded dreams.

><

All of Ermoupolis was in fact a kind of museum: a quirky, obscure one, rather than the institutional kind. It was not a fate foreseen by the refugees who conceived of Ermoupolis as a beacon, designed to declare to the world that a new Greece had been born. They were so successful that the city they raised from the stones was later dubbed 'a miracle'. It was built from a peculiar blend of entrepreneurial and nationalist zeal, as its name reflects: Ermoupolis derives from Hermes, the ancient god of trade.

At first the refugees came from the islands of Chios and Psara, both of which were sites of atrocities during the 'Sacred Struggle', the name the survivors gave to the Greek War of Independence. They also came from Asia Minor, and later from all over Greece.

Syros was neutral ground, under French protection. A community of Capuchin monks had settled there in 1633, followed shortly after by Jesuits. During the war it was considered a safe haven, though nominally the island remained under the rule of the Turks. The French protection, along with the island's deep harbour and its central position in the Cyclades, made Syros the most important shipping and commercial centre in the country.

As its settlers acquired wealth and influence, they built a city that expressed their mood of optimism and importance. Stone mansions rose on the waterfront, their foundations in the sea like the palaces in Venice. With them came a model for a new society: orphanages and poor houses were erected, along with a hospital and elaborate churches. The refugees created a grand and peaceful place; the streets of Ermoupolis are cool, elegant and pervaded by an architectural calm.

But the city harbours an illusional world. Within the mansions, the walls were painted to look like marble, friezes of neo-classical busts were painted to look like stone relief and ceilings were painted to imitate elaborate plaster moulding. One of the town's showpieces, the Apollon Theatre, was designed to resemble a temple of illusion, La Scala in Milan. In the same way, the site of the city bears little relationship to the surrounding geography. In the gaps between the mansions one can occasionally catch glimpses of the sea. Every time I saw that band of blue

I was surprised to be reminded that, yes, here I was, on the Aegean.

The city's glory days lasted until the turn of the century. What had made it a wonder – that refugees had raised it on a rock – also proved to be its limitation, and eventually its downfall. Ermoupolis was proposed as the capital of the new Greece – but could Greece be ruled from a rock in the sea? When the Corinth Canal was completed in 1893, much of the European shipping that had once passed through Syros now circumvented it. And so the island's decline began.

Ermoupolis is shot through with a sense of loss. In the streets surrounding the Greek Orthodox cathedral of Agios Nicholas, for instance, 'For Sale' signs hang in the boarded windows. The steps linking the steep streets have been broken by weeds. Carefully preserved homes stand next to ruins. The Apollon's last performance took place in 1953; restoration work on the building began in 1970, but remains unfinished. An atmosphere of decay, or of brave failure, has become part of the city's texture. Despite it, however, Ermoupolis remains an improvement on nature. Its streets protect you from the relentless stoniness that characterises the rest of Syros.

After a few days on the island I chose to turn my back on its bleakness and remain in the city. During the hot afternoons I swam at a pebbly beach on the edge of town, along with city matrons who smoked as they lay in their turbans and matching bathing suits. The arid landscape was leavened by the masonry arches at the base of the houses that stood over the sea. Across the water rose the holy island of Tinos, its steep hills softened and partly obscured by the heat haze of the Greek summer.

><

As Ermoupolis rose and fell, a different type of miracle was taking place on Tinos, the third point in the triangle of islands. In 1822 a nun called Pelagia, an inhabitant of Tinos's Convent of Kechrovounio, dreamt that an icon of the Virgin Mary was concealed on the island. The icon of the Panagia Evangelistria, or Our Lady of Good Tidings, was found where Pelagia's dream said it would be hidden, and the discovery was held to be a good omen in the War of Independence. Miraculous cures were soon attributed to the icon and an Orthodox cathedral was built on the site where it had been found. The significance of the icon is manifold and says much about the Greek sense of national destiny. March 25, the day of the Annunciation, when Mary heard the good tidings about the son she would bear, is also the country's national day; on that day in 1821 the Sacred Struggle officially began.

The devout and the afflicted still flock to Tinos. On 25 March and on the Feast of the Assumption on 15 August, there are so many worshippers that they cannot all find beds, and so they have to sleep on the streets. When Prime Minister Andreas Papandreou was fighting for his life in hospital in December 1995, holy water from Tinos was taken to his bedside.

An equilateral triangle of miracles. The white marble used to build the church of the Panagia Evangelistria includes material recycled from the Delian Temple of Apollo.

><

Privately, I had begun to dub Syros 'the island of work'. In the shops, the post office and the banks, the islanders worked efficiently and without fuss. Conversations were direct and to the point, a far cry from the nosy chitchat I'd become accustomed to elsewhere in Greece. And the true heart of Ermoupolis was not Miaouli Square but the city's working port. It was best seen at sunrise, when the still water turned silver and gold, or in the evening, when sailors cruising the Cyclades had tied up their yachts. Then the tables on the surrounding streets were full and the shadows in the water slithered like dolphins.

The port was dominated by the dry dock and floating crane of the Neorion shipyard. At night, the yard was covered in lights and I could see the shadowy figures of men working when I dined at the harbourside taverns. The shipyard was the oldest in Greece. Its existence – serious and unaesthetic – was the most visible sign that the islanders had managed to cling to the work ethic that had built Ermoupolis. The yard worked a twenty-four-hour roster, every day of the year. After only a few days on Syros I no longer thought of the yard as a blot on the harbour, but found myself checking regularly on the progress of the paint job on the great Norwegian freighter in the dry dock.[†]

Tourists found the shipyard off-putting, but Panayiotis Boutouris, who owned a travel agency at the port, said he counted that a blessing. "We are not an island of waiters." Syros was fortunate enough to have an independent life. Its tavernas were open all year round, in contrast to those on Mykonos, the island's rival and spectre across the water, which closed down for the winter.

Boutouris was, fittingly, a brisk, busy man. I had been told that he would be able to tell me anything I wanted to know about the island, and, as if to confirm this, a big, English-language sign hung in his office: *We can handle anything.* You could imagine him hanging the sign himself.

I met him in the early evening. He led me outside to a table overlooking the port and the shipyard, lit a cigar and genially told me his story. In 1960, when tourism was beginning to flourish on Mykonos, Syros was poor. When he was eighteen, Boutouris went to sea because it was the only work he could find. He sailed to China, to Thailand and to North Korea, working for the most part on old, slow cargo boats and in inefficient ports. Then he landed a job on a well-run cruiser, the *Laconia*. But disaster struck when the ship caught fire, all 22,000 tonnes of her, in rough seas north of Madeira. Escaping from the ship was the unforgettable adventure of his youth. "I saw it burn from a lifeboat. You cannot imagine. I felt like Nero."

When Boutouris married, he stopped sailing and settled on Syros. He worked in the shipyard for a short time before leaving to start up his agency, which catered to the overflow from the other Cycladic islands and those few who deliberately sought Syros out. Many visitors found the island disappointing, he observed drily, because it did not have whitewashed houses, like the postcards.

"I am proud of the island. I like to be autonomous and so does Syros. That fits." Boutouris smiled expansively as he looked around the port. He had a good life, he was lucky, but then again working on an island had its costs, it wasn't always easy. "It's beautiful now, isn't it?" he said. "But we pay for this, we pay."

What did he mean? The air was as warm as breath, and the sea was utterly still: as still as yoghurt, the Greeks say, as still as olive oil. He asked me if I had children, and I told him about my son, Dylan. Boutouris said he had been married for thirteen years before his wife had conceived. She had twins – a boy and a girl – but they were born prematurely, during a storm, in the seventh month of her pregnancy. The island hospital was not equipped to care for the babies and they had to be transferred to Athens as quickly as possible. And here was the cost of island life, for how could his babies leave Syros in a storm?

Boutouris was a sailor and a resourceful man. *We can handle anything.* He hired a tugboat, a vessel that was stable enough to take him and his children to Mykonos, the closest island with an airstrip; from there, a Hercules aircraft would fly him and the babies to Athens. It was a good plan and would have worked, but fate intervened. One of the tug's engines failed, and instead of taking an hour, the journey to Mykonos took three. The oxygen that had been keeping his son alive ran out, and the boy died.

><

In a short time I had become accustomed to the rhythms of Ermoupolis; it was tempting to imagine simply staying on in the odd little city. I peered into the tumbledown mansions for sale and daydreamed about refurbishing one. Ermoupolis impressed me as an honest and dignified Aegean survivor; I dreaded what lay ahead. Many of my fellow guests at the pension were attending a United Nations conference, enigmatically entitled the Anthropology of Space. Despite their earnest attention, Ermoupolis still gave the impression that it was a secret metropolis, forgotten and undiscovered. Another illusion.

The little old man at my pension had somehow divined my misgivings, and told me, without irony, that the reason I was content to linger on Syros was because it was the best island in Greece. All further travel was bound to disappoint. "Stay here," he urged.

But it was time for me to leave. On my last day I decided to splurge on a book: a heavy, illustrated volume on Ermoupolis that I had seen in a bookshop. Before I could buy it, however, the proprietor, Mr Stathis Stathopoulos, a white-haired, gentle man in his seventies, insisted that I take the book to the post office to be weighed. It would be folly to travel with such a tome, he said, and he wanted me to make sure I could afford to post it on to my father's village in the Peloponnese. "And don't forget to ask for registered mail . . ."

When I returned, Mr Stathopoulos took me upstairs to show me his renovations: he had converted the upper storey of his shop into a salon and reading room. The shop had been operating since 1912. At one time it had also been a publishing house, but all that had stopped during the Second World War, when Greece was occupied by the Germans and the Italians.

I knew that Syros had suffered greatly in the war because so little food was grown there. The island had paid a terrible price for the imbalance at the heart of Ermoupolis – for the size of its dreams. What did Mr Stathopoulos remember of the Occupation?

The old man did not retreat from the question, but it affected his demeanour. With a shift of his shoulders, he became more remote and impersonal. Even his voice changed timbre: it steadied and took on a more formal tone.

He had been eighteen when the Occupation began. "Syros suffered more than anywhere in Greece. It was an industrial place, you see. People were involved in making things, in shipping and such. Children died in the street. They fell like flies. Their stomachs swelled up and they died." He pointed past the shop window to the street outside, as though to indicate that there, in a place just beyond our range of vision, was where the children had fallen.[‡]

The Italians arrived on Syros in 1941, and took over from the

Germans. The English bombed the island daily, so that the Italians could not leave. They held concerts, they played music. They were not warlike, but the famine occurred under Italian rule nevertheless.

"They let us starve . . . They would eat on a balcony," and Mr Stathopoulos pointed towards Miaouli Square, "and the children would gather under it while they ate, waiting for them to shake out their tablecloths. And then the children would fight for the scraps, and the Italians would look down and laugh."

All the same, he preferred the Italians to the Germans. "The Germans killed children. If they caught a child stealing, they would kill him."

He sighed deeply. He knew of islanders who had sold all their property in order to keep eating. "They sold their houses for food. There was a flourishing black market, it traded openly. Someone sold a mansion in this town for three gold coins so he could buy onions and potatoes."

After the Occupation came the civil war, and "after the civil war it still wasn't over. The people in the Resistance were sent to Makronissos and such places.[§] There came a time in Greece when we were not even allowed to sell books."

A look of weary disgust crossed his face. Then the telephone rang – an enquiry about an order – and we were returned to the present day. But the emotions that the old man had conjured up still hung in the air, and I instinctively felt that they would disperse more quickly if I left him alone. I thanked him and made for the door, but he called me back.

"Write about my new reading room," he said. "Write about how I have improved my bookshop."

Outside the heat persisted. Mr Stathopoulos's story had disturbed me and I regretted having asked him to tell it. At the fish and fruit market near the square I bought some food for lunch: a bag of pistachios, some white peaches and two ripe tomatoes; I would eat them on the balcony before swimming in the afternoon.

I walked back to the pension, thankfully diving into the shadows thrown by the cool stone of the buildings that had risen so improbably and yet so gracefully from a sour rock on the Aegean.

* From *Sacred Geography of the Ancient Greeks* by Jean Richer. Richer's English translator, Christine Rhone, became interested in him because of her scholarly research into the astrological symbolism in Plato's *Republic* and *Laws*. In Plato's ideal state, the inhabitants and the land were divided into a dozen parts, each one named after a 'zodiacal deity'. Rhone writes that seen from the air, Plato's republic would resemble a twelve-spoked wheel, similar to the zodiacal wheels that Richer drew over the Aegean.

† The Neorion shipyard was established during the boom days of Ermoupolis and is the only shipyard still operating on the island. A group of managers from shipyards around Greece purchased the yard after its previous owner, the Greek Government, closed it down because it could not run it at a profit. At the time of my visit, the yard employed 500 people and was touted as a model of privatisation. The company's president, Mr Nikolas Tavoularis, told me that in reviving

the yard, he was not simply motivated by money. "I like to make things work," he said.

‡ In 1939 the number of deaths on the island was 435; in 1942 the figure had risen sharply to 2290, the bodies being interred in a large ditch on the outskirts of Ermoupolis. (Information taken from *Inside Hitler's Greece* by Mark Mazower.)

§ Makronissos is the infamous island where suspected leftists were imprisoned and tortured.

CHAPTER TWO

THE SHATTERED ISLAND

T HE LITTLE CHURCH was near the windmill, on a clifftop at the edge of town. I had spent an hour walking through narrow streets, past chichi boutiques, whitewashed cave houses, construction sites and uncleared rubble from the earthquake of '56. I was willing myself to be seduced by Oia's beauty. But Oia was too incoherent, too disparate; its streets saddened me. The church door was open and so I went inside, hoping for a moment's grace.

The old lady was slumped over a table at the entrance, her long grey hair gathered in a loose knot. "*Herete*," I said. "Be happy." At the sound of my voice she raised her head and turned her face towards me. "*Herete*," she answered. Her eyes looked damaged, perhaps by cataracts. I wondered what she was doing in the church; she hadn't been praying – no candles had been lit – nor was she collecting money. "I have been resting," she said, "the heat has made me tired." I turned to leave, but she asked me to please stay and sit with her for a while.

It was better not to go outside, she said. The neighbourhood was too stony, and the buildings were damaged and ugly. It was a penance to be in such a place. She came from Apano Meria, the upper place, not this godforsaken hole. Her face brightened when she mentioned the name of her home – did I know it? Had I been there? It was so beautiful. A central place, with a central road that led around the town and back to the square again. Her hands traced a loop in the air to show me the shape of the road. Sailors lived there, and captains had built fine houses.

"Where is Apano Meria?" I asked her.

"In Oia," she said angrily, "in Oia, of course." I took this to mean that it was a neighbourhood of Oia, or perhaps an adjoining village. She had gone to church there and had known the liturgy by heart, she told me. She had been a good housewife. Now, nobody cared for these things or for what she knew. Her husband had died and her son was lost to her. That was her misfortune, to have had only one child, and for the child to have been a son.

The blind woman could not tell me why she was in the church that day, she could not tell me what she was waiting for.

"People are fools," she said.

"Why do you say that?"

"Because I am about to die. Everything is written, don't you know that? We cannot escape our fate. That is why I am in this place now, this stony place. That is why I am no longer in Apano Meria." And again she told me about the road and the houses, her hands making the shape of the road. Its church of Agios

Dimitri was splendid. Surely I knew it.

The church we were sitting in had a dome over the iconostasis. Its silver-encrusted icon of a saint on horseback looked like the traditional representation of St Dimitri. But when I asked the old lady where she lived, she repeated the story about Apano Meria. "Stay with me," she said, whenever I stood up to go; and I did stay for a time, hoping that someone would come to take her home. Someone must know where she is, I reasoned. Someone must have led her here, and opened the church for her.

A dinner engagement meant I finally had to leave her. As I walked back through Oia, I looked for the place she had described, but could not find the looping road of Apano Meria. Later I learned that I had been there all along: Apano Meria was the old name for Oia itself. The old lady had become an exile in her own town.

><

I had travelled to Thira by hydrofoil – the Greeks call them flying dolphins – because the ferry I needed left Syros at midnight. The dolphin stopped at five other Cycladic islands before arriving at Thira, the end of the line. It lurched along so noisily, it was like sailing the Aegean in a bus.

Despite the length of the journey, the choppy sea and the inescapable diesel fumes, I began to feel a knot of excitement as we approached Thira. (Most people, Greeks and tourists alike, still call the island Santorini, but it has officially been renamed Thira; part of a confusing reversion to ancient place names that has taken place all over the country.) The dolphin had filled with tourists – British, Germans, Americans – and the talk was of the island we were heading for. "We went there for the day last week," said a British woman, "and I thought it was so magical we just had to go back and stay. It's like nowhere else in the world." Another passenger, a quiet, soft-voiced boy, also told me that the island was one of a kind: "You should see it at least once." He was from Ikaria, the island where Icarus is said to have plunged into the sea, and he brightened when I was able to place his home as one of the islands in the north-eastern Aegean. He had met Greeks who had not heard of it. "Not many people go there," he said. "Perhaps you would like it."

We stopped talking when Thira came into view. It deserved to be seen in silence. Photography does not do Thira justice, any more than a photograph of the Alps can tell you what the Eiger is like. At their best, photographs capture a mood, a gesture – one aspect of a view – and in doing so they can hint at a more complex whole. But some sights are so immense, not only in size but in the impact they have on us, that they elude photography. My guess is that of all the islands of the Aegean, Thira is the most photographed. But I have yet to see a photograph that captures the surprising power of Thira, its capacity to shock.

My first impression was of towering black, grey and brown cliffs, rising sheer from the sea. Giant mounds of scree were heaped at their base, and there were tiny, irregular blocks of white clustered on the clifftops: unlikely dwellings in a lunar landscape. Later, I wrote in my journal that it looked like a movie set of an island at the end of the world.

Thira is roughly crescent-shaped. The dolphin was now approaching the port of Athinios, plying its way across the great bowl that forms the inner curve of the crescent. This expanse, the chief wonder of the island, is called the caldera. It was formed by the volcanic explosion that is thought to have destroyed

Minoan civilisation some 3500 years ago. As we entered the caldera, the sea became calm for the first time that morning; it also appeared to change colour, becoming an intense, ethereal blue. Some say the colour is due to the depth of the sea here – 380 metres – or it may be an illusion caused by the contrast with the framing black cliffs. Whatever the cause, this blueness and stillness combined to give the impression that we were somehow entering a zone of heightened reality.

And then we landed. The port, a level platform surrounded by cliffs, was hellishly hot and crowded. As I disembarked, a German tourist gave my suitcase a savage kick, something I preferred to do myself. I boarded a crowded bus that zigzagged wildly around hairpin bends to the clifftop and then lurched on to the town of Fira, the island's capital. The bus driver scowled at my case and my questions; he held all tourists in contempt. From Fira another bus veered along a precipice to take me to Oia, a town at the north-western end of the crescent. The bus to Oia was full, and as I swung from a strap, I listened to despondent English conversations about the high cost of island bus travel. "I already hate this place," I heard someone say.

In Oia, I went to the tourist office and stood in line to find a room, too exhausted to complain. I shared some grapes with an American woman from Philadelphia who was also searching for a place to sleep. A stiff wind blew through the open door, another irritation. The American woman sighed: "Travel sucks, doesn't it?"

The prize rooms in Oia are crowded along the cliff face overlooking the caldera. The room I was given was not one of these; it was situated at the back of the crescent, away from the main town. I made the mistake of taking a taxi there, and discovered too late that it was a two-minute walk from the bus stop. The driver, unembarrassed, charged me 2000 drachmas and accused me of wanting to snatch the bread from the mouths of his children when I refused to pay.

As I slammed the door of the cab I was greeted by Irini, the owner of my new room. She gave me a sweet smile of welcome, and offered me coffee and homemade biscuits. From *poniria* to kindness again; the swift transitions could take your breath away.

My room was quiet and clean. It looked out over a vineyard and terraced fields to the ocean, where a tall, white-sailed ship was slipping away. Only on Thira could such a view be considered second-rate.

><

Every day, in a different way, Thira continued to be hellish. I found little bubbles of harmony and quiet there but never recovered from my initial impression that tourism had made the island sick. Visitors are drawn to Thira by its extraordinary geography, and here was a strange symmetry: a destructive event had created an awful beauty, and that beauty was now the cause of the island's demise. Where once Thira was buried in ash, it was now seduced by gold.

The next day I took a bus back to the city of Fira. The road wound along the island's narrow spine: to the right was the caldera, the water a deep, misty cobalt; to the left were terraced fields, the abandoned legacy of farmers who for centuries had coaxed sustenance from the pumice-strewn soil. Now the terraces were slowly crumbling, losing their definition, their history; a vast, fallow stairway falling towards the sea.

Fira was noisy, and covered in ugly signs in English: *Bagels!*

Just like New York; Alexander the Great's Macedonian Cuisine; Apocalypse Night Club – Live Show, Hot, Hot, Hot; Santorini I Love You Restaurant. The swank part of town was the strip overlooking the caldera, where gift shops sold hand-painted icons and gold reproductions of Mycenaean and Minoan jewellery. A cable car negotiated the steep descent to the sea here, travelling over a donkey track. Classical music spilled out from stylish cafes; you could listen to Pachelbel's Canon while drinking an overpriced espresso and gazing at the caldera, the sight that held all this commerce in thrall.

Roughly in the centre of the caldera were the Kameni, or 'burnt islands'. From a distance they looked like slag heaps, but they were islands in embryo and still volcanically active. The Kameni have been rising from the sea and sinking back again since the explosion that first shattered Thira – the greatest volcanic explosion known to history.

><

"No, of course I never get sick of the view," said Rita. She was an architect, a young, rather fierce woman from northern Greece. Her office had wide views of the caldera and the shops and cafes that clung to the cliffs on its rim. She told me that this honeycomb of development was structurally unsafe and in danger of falling into the water. Workers were attempting to strengthen the site by underpinning it with a platform of steel and rocks, but she couldn't really say whether this would make it earthquake-proof.

Yes, settlement was precarious on Thira, said Rita, but so it was throughout the Aegean. Not all the problems were seismological. The place was remote, buffeted by winds, and both wood and water were scarce. It was heroic that the islanders had survived there at all.

Rita drew me a diagram of a traditional Thiran home. The islanders no longer built them, but they were ingenious constructions. How do you build a house without wood, or water for bricks or mortar? The islanders dug cave houses into the soft volcanic rock, and lived in the sides of cliffs and mountains. Some of their dwellings have survived in Oia. The underground houses were cool in the summer, warm in the winter; there was no need to burn wood for heat. And the houses were camouflaged from the pirates who for hundreds of years were another blight on island life.

Rita was smiling as she drew. The resilience and inventiveness of the people who had built such houses pleased her. She had plans to marry, and had designed a house for herself and her husband in which some of the rooms would be partly excavated from the side of a hill, in the traditional style. She told me that the freestanding outer rooms of the folk houses had low, domed roofs made from a mixture of mud, pumice and dried tomato plants.

Dried tomato plants?

"This is a barren place," she said, enjoying my surprise. "The islanders used whatever was at hand."

We talked about tourism's stranglehold on the island. Like most Greeks she felt ambivalent about the phenomenon. Tourism had brought ease for the first time in centuries; it was no surprise that it had been embraced with such zeal. Rarely did communities choose subsistence farming over cash profits; cash was winning, not just on Thira but all over the world.

Later that evening I talked to Andoni and Irini, the owners of my room. They had both grown up in Oia but had left for Athens shortly after the '56 earthquake. Now, in their retirement, they came back to rent out their rooms for the summer.

"The earthquake didn't drive us out of Oia," said Irini crossly in reply to my question. Visitors to Thira developed an obsession with natural calamities, she complained. They forgot that all of Greece was an earthquake zone. No, it was mundane poverty that had caused them to leave. Life had been too hard, although Andoni said that he missed the old routines.

Once, all of September had been devoted to crushing the grapes for the famous local wine, the only commercial crop still grown on the island. He remembered carts leaving Oia piled high with tiny tomatoes. I had seen tomatoes growing in private gardens, and like the stunted grapevines in Andoni's vineyard, they looked, to my untrained eye, to be pitiful specimens. But the shrunken fruit were famous for the intensity of their flavour, I learnt. The tomatoes had once been made into tomato paste; the island had supported nine canning factories, but they had all closed now. Thira's days of productive manual work were almost over; even its pumice mines had been shut down. According to Andoni, there were only four or five farmers left in Oia, and they were like him, just hobby farmers mucking around.

Andoni was a builder and he couldn't say that he missed the cave dwellings that most of the villagers had lived in when he was a child. As soon as they could afford to do so, his neighbours had moved to freestanding homes, reserving the dark, unventilated caves for stabling their animals. Now – and he gave a sardonic laugh – tourists lived in them. The cave houses didn't even have bathrooms.

This remark caused Irini to rise from her seat, agitated by the suggestion that hygiene standards had been lower in the old days. "That's not right, don't listen to him!"

"Well, you tell me who had a bathroom then?" asked Andoni. But Irini was walking off into the kitchen. A glare was her only reply.

><

In Oia the sunset draws such crowds that twilight has become a theatrical event: Tourism of the Absurd. Every evening during the season, people race from the bus stop to the western edge of town, clutching their cameras. They wander around Oia in the afternoon, asking where the sun goes down. They vie for rooms with sunset views; on other islands I heard travellers talk about their desire to 'see the sunset' on Thira. In Oia I cavesdropped on a Greek couple calling Athens on their mobile phone. They were touring the Cyclades; of all the sights they had seen, none could match the Oia sunset. Words failed them.

Oia is less vulgar than Fira, but the tourism is as intense. Craft and jewellery shops are crammed next to piano bars and patisseries. The streets are narrow, and at twilight, when the crowd arrives, they are claustrophobic. While the sun set I found myself standing near a group of disaffected Greek-Americans who, like me, were dividing their attention between the sun and its admirers. No-one talked about it, but their contempt for the scene was palpable; it hung between us in the rosy air. One of them, a strikingly handsome man, was married to a cheerful American woman with an enormous bosom. She wasn't particularly taken by the sunset, but she wasn't bothered by the crowd either. She smiled at her husband.

"You know, honey," she said, "I want to come back to Oia, and do you know what I want to do?"

He didn't answer, so she continued: "I'd like to shop."

The man looked away from the woman and said evenly, "I'm not coming with you."

"Why not?"

"Because I'm never coming to this place again."

A week later I watched the sunset from a ferry as it pulled out of Paros. Lovely stuff, but no-one cared. The Paros sunset does not advertise.

><

Akrotiri is a small village at the opposite end of Thira's crescent from Oia. Here, under layers of pumice and ash, lie the oldest remains of the island's human past.

Archaeologist Spyridon Marinatos began the excavations at Akrotiri in 1967, searching for Atlantis. He chose to dig in the fissured earth on the southern tip of the island, the point closest to Crete. Before its destruction, Thira was round, fertile and known as Kalliste, meaning 'the most beautiful'. Marinatos uncovered an abandoned town preserved under pumice and ash, multi-storey villas decorated with wall paintings, equipped with running water and flushing toilets. The plumbing, the style of the pottery and the paintings all indicated strong links with the Minoan people of Crete.*

The bus dropped me off at the archaeological site, near the beach on the outskirts of Akrotiri. At most ancient Greek sites the setting is crucial; the landscape and the architecture are inseparable and in harmony. But at Akrotiri the site exists despite the upheavals of the land around it. This is where Thira meets Kalliste.

The diggings, some of them twenty metres deep, were concealed beneath a vast corrugated-iron and fibreglass shed. Only one-thirtieth of the town had been uncovered, forty buildings in all; of these, only three had been fully investigated.

I followed an animated Greek guide who was keeping a group of English-speaking tourists enthralled. As usual I had neglected to book myself on to a tour, but this time I regretted it. More than most sites, Akrotiri needs decoding; all the untrained eye can see is the dusty shells of the three-storey buildings and the scaffolding barriers between them.

Neat piles of storage jars filled a corner of the shed. Eighty thousand of them had been found so far, the guide said, but not a single skeleton had come to light. In one home, clay tablets covered in script were discovered on a small table; useful clues, if only someone knew how to read them. Did the residents manage to escape, or is a pile of their bones yet to be discovered? How important was the settlement? Who lived there? Nobody knew, but wonderful theories abounded: that beneath the rubble lay the remains of what was literally a Golden Age, or perhaps the lost matriarchy of the ancient world; that the Thiran dust cloud was responsible for the seven plagues of Egypt described in Exodus; that the survivors fled to the Holy Land, where they were known as the Philistines . . .

The settlement's most evocative legacies are the wall frescoes found on the upper storey of every house uncovered so far. They have been painstakingly restored and are on display in the National Archaeological Museum in Athens. The paintings use space and colour boldly; figures are drawn with supple, vigorous lines, painted with a graceful economy that appears artless but is not. A fisherman holds his catch, two boys box, a fleet sets sail. The wall paintings of women in the so-called House of the

Ladies are particularly striking and enigmatic. The women have long, dark hair, bare breasts and wear waisted, flowing skirts. Here is a proud womanhood, a love of beauty, a love of nature. The images beg the question: what kind of people would decorate their homes with work such as this?

The Greek guide smiled at her audience and told them that if they wanted to know the answers to such questions they would have to wait 100 years: that was how long it would take the experts to sift through a more substantial portion of the site and decipher whatever clues it might hold.

><

At the bus station, the sight of my fellow travellers filled me with a misanthropic gloom. The vulgarity everywhere evident in Fira had affected its visitors as well. A type of collective madness appeared to have overtaken them; or it may simply have been the effect of the heat. The girl in the bikini top, shorts and running shoes was lissome enough to carry it off, but most of the women around her were not: a white-haired lady from Germany wore a yellow T-shirt and bright pink hot pants, an elderly English woman in a singlet had pushed her thin white leggings up to the knee. Were they wearing someone else's clothes, or did they dress like this at home? They looked red-faced and uneasy. And where had all these baseball caps come from? These dreadlocks and cut-off army fatigues? I sat on the steps outside the bus office, sullen and superior, and joined the bus drivers in their habitual sneer at the crowd.

"Tourism is like a sickness here," I said to one of the drivers. He nodded moodily in reply. He had come to Thira twenty years ago to help build the airport, had married a local girl and stayed on. He preferred his home town, a village near Thessaloniki in northern Greece.

"On Thira, money has taken the place of human contact," he said. "Everyone is interested in making as much money as they can. In the place I was born, people want to talk to you, to have a meal with you, to find out about you. They are not like that here . . ."

He also disliked the island winters, when the shops and tavernas shut down; he was resentful that the island had such a tenuous hold on an independent life. I wondered aloud if islanders had more time for each other in the winter. "It makes no difference," said the driver. "They want to buy big cars, and to go on holidays to France."

I had been reading *The Greeks*, Professor Kitto's classic work on ancient Greece. His sure, clear prose is imbued with a yearning for the past, and this tapped into my own dissatisfaction. 'A sense of the wholeness of things is perhaps the most typical feature of the Greek mind', wrote Kitto. 'The modern mind divides, specialises, thinks in categories: the Greek instinct was the opposite, to take the widest view, to see things as an organic whole.'

A sense of the wholeness of things – that had been lost on Thira. The island lacked balance, it no longer felt grounded. A traditional way of life had been abandoned in a sudden movement. And in that movement, the connections that had defined island life, connections with the land and with the community, had been severed. It was a familiar story, even an understandable one. The trouble was that I didn't like the circus that had come to fill the vacuum.

I decided to go on to Ancient Thira, a Greek and Byzantine

settlement on the mountaintop of Mesa Vouno. The bus stopped at a suburban street, where a signpost pointed to a towering stone peak directly above. I could see pine trees growing on the slopes and a tiny whitewashed church clinging to the side of the rock. The trees and the church reminded me of my father's village; a cheering and calming sight. And so I began to climb.

The afternoon air was cool, and although the gradient was steep, it was not unmanageable. A minibus timetable told me that the last bus to the ancient site left at two o'clock. It was now four. I had no intention of climbing to the summit: it looked far too high.

But the walk was exhilarating. I liked the view of the beach from the mountain. The black sand was swept neatly, in the European style, and the beach umbrellas stood like soldiers in formation. I passed a German couple walking down the road; the woman's hair was wet with sweat. I asked them how far it was to the ancient town. "All the way to the top," gasped the woman. The rocky peak loomed above us, looking like a place where eagles nested. "It's too far," I said. They suggested I hitch a ride; soon after, a hire car and two mopeds passed me, but they didn't stop. I kept walking.

I realised that this was the first time I had felt happy on Thira. I was finally alone in a quiet, beautiful place and my body wanted to stretch out, to keep going. Soon my face and legs were perspiring freely from the effort. I looped my skirt up and climbed, occasionally stopping to catch my breath and to take in the view. I passed a tall, narrow cave in the rock and cool stands of pine trees. The further I climbed, the happier I felt. I had given up all thought of hitching now.

When I eventually made it to the top I found a car park, an ice-cream truck that was closed for business and a dour Italian girl in running shoes and a yellow bikini. I smiled at her, expecting some sign of congratulation in return, but she looked disdainfully at my red, perspiring face and continued to smoke her cigarette. A narrow track led to the archaeological site, but the gate had been locked for the day and a barbed-wire fence prevented trespassers.

A Norwegian on a moped asked me if I had walked up, and when I nodded he applauded and offered me some water. He was staying at Perissa, a seaside town on the other side of Mesa Vouno, he said; when I turned to walk back down the mountain he offered me a lift. His kindness and the cool wind on my face and legs were a fine reward for my climb.

That evening, I ate dinner at a green cafe that perched over the caldera. Whenever I looked out to sea, the image of that sulky Italian beauty kept coming back to me. There was no escaping the face of the spoiler who mocked and was mocked during the season on Thira.

* Marinatos believed that the legend of Atlantis fused two events: the destruction of Thira and the decline of the Minoans. After the volcano erupted, the culture of the Mediterranean regressed. The Minoans lost their impetus; some went to Mycenae on the Peloponnese – a less advanced community – which became the pre-eminent Greek city. But subsequent settlements in Greece continued to move away

from the Minoan standard, and the country became more and more primitive. From about 1200 BC a 'Dark Age' of illiteracy and artistic and technological decline took hold, lasting for 400 years.

Scholars do not know why the Minoans were unable to pick up the pieces after the disaster. No traces of their fleet have ever been found, and it is speculated that the tidal waves also destroyed the shipyards and the shipwrights who worked in them.

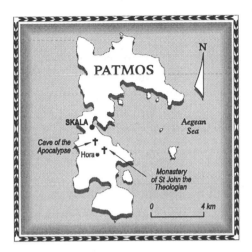

CHAPTER THREE

THE ISLAND OF THE APOCALYPSE

C IRCUMVENTIONS ARE typical of the Greek ferry system: the logic governing the routes is impenetrable, the timetable information is unreliable and the seas are capricious. To travel from Thira in the south to Patmos in the north-east I had to backtrack to Paros in the west and wait there for four hours. An eastbound vessel left Paros in the late afternoon, and was due to arrive at Patmos after midnight. Winds had gusted over Thira for almost every day of my stay; I had been dreading the day at sea.

And then the wind dropped. As the boat set out I remembered why I loved the islands. I blessed the ferries of Greece for forcing me to spend a day on the Aegean. I had no choice; when you least expect it, happiness comes. I was a passenger, and I sat back, my feet on the rail, suspended in a universe of blueness.

In Greece, during the good weather, the sea is a dense indigo, absorbing all the colour that the ruthless noonday sun blanches from the sky. The glare turns the horizon white, and the sky disappears into the water. On bright days the sea contains such a superabundance of blue that the waves look as solidly dark as a dye.

I had nothing to do that day but be buoyed by that sea. On the ferry from Paros, wanting to savour the day for as long as possible, I remained on deck looking out over the water until the sea and sky were black. By then the deck lights were bright enough to read by, so I put on my coat and began writing a letter to a friend.

A group of men were huddled by the cabin door, smoking cigarettes.

"What are you writing?" one of them called out.

"It's my own business," I answered, and the man sighed.

"All we want to do is pass the time," he said. "What can we do on a boat?"

I felt reproached; forgot about it, and returned to my letter. When I finished I read back over what I'd written, and smiled at the jokes. One of the men jumped up.

"Now she's laughing. My God! Tell me what you're laughing about! I'm dying of boredom here."

He was tall, open-faced and dark-haired. He strode up to me and pulled up a chair. "Talk to me," he said.

His name was Pano. He and his companions worked for the Greek National Tourist Organisation and were heading for Patmos to help prepare for next week's grand festivities.

What festivities?

This time, it was Pano who laughed. "All the world is going

there, even the Pope, or so they say. How can you not know about it?"

He told me that Patmos was preparing to commemorate the 1900th anniversary of the writing of the Book of Revelation. A celebration of the Apocalypse, no less. St John mentions the island in Revelations (1:9): 'I John, who also am your brother, and companion in tribulation, and in the kingdom and patience of Jesus Christ, was in the isle that is called Patmos, for the word of God, and for the testimony of Jesus Christ'.

The more I thought about the celebration, the more paradoxical it seemed. In almost two millennia St John's apocalyptic prophecy had not been fulfilled; that could be seen as a cause for celebration, but how could believers take part without repudiating their faith? Conversely, if the prophecy *did* come to pass, a celebration would hardly be appropriate.

"How strange," I said.

Pano agreed, but for different reasons. "I am not one for religion," he said. "Once we believed in the twelve gods of Olympus and built temples everywhere. Then we stopped believing in that and believed in one God only. Why? Who is right? Were our ancestors bigger fools than us?"

Neither of us knew the answer and we both laughed as though the matter of faith were a simple riddle and not the unfathomable mystery of the ages. Lights shone in the distance. "That's Patmos ahead," said a sailor. Way out to sea, the lights rose asymmetrically over a dark, steeply rising mound that was barely distinguishable against the velvet sky; there were signs of life and warmth on the island of the Apocalypse.

><

Soon after we landed, the wind began to blow again. It rattled the shutters of my room and howled through the trees in the garden below. In the morning, it had not abated. I stood on my narrow balcony, having secured the window to stop it slamming, and looked down at the beach behind my hotel: a small, lonely cove with cliffs on two sides. Further out, birds circled a tiny white island; beyond it I could see the dark outline of Ikaria.

I had previously visited Patmos with my husband, Tony, who'd had a terrible dream on his first night on the island. A plague had come, killing thousands upon thousands. There was no known cure. People fell ill and died afraid. The dream's final image was of a child, wracked with pain, begging for death. Tony had woken not knowing whether he had the courage to kill the child or the fortitude to listen to his pitiful screaming. He'd wondered why such a dream had come to him; I'd suggested that he must have been thinking about St John's prophecy, as plague is one of the Four Horsemen of the Apocalypse.* But Tony had insisted that no, he hadn't known the details of the prophecy. You must have, I'd replied, everybody hears about it at some time. The nightmare of ending was written on Patmos. That's why you dreamt it. He'd remained unconvinced.

><

When St John wrote the Book of Revelations, the island was his prison. He was exiled on Patmos in 95 AD by the Roman emperor Domitian, the first emperor who demanded that he be called 'God the Lord'. Almost a thousand years later, in 1088, a Byzantine monk, the Blessed Christodoulos, founded the Monastery of St John the Theologian on Patmos, which he described as 'this island at the edge of the world'. The monastery he built resembles a great stone castle, rising severely on the hill that overlooks the port.

Christodoulos's labours transformed Patmos from a stony desert island to a place of wealth and influence in the Greek Orthodox world. After his death in 1093, his body became a holy relic and miraculous cures were attributed to it.[†]

St John's esoteric and doom-laden prophecy has been good for Patmos. The island's streets, houses and fields look orderly, prosperous and harmonious, an impression made keener because of the preparations for the Apocalypse party. Fresh tarmac had been laid on the road near my hotel and the scaffolding was slowly coming down from outside the newly painted post office, a Moorish-inspired folly.

In Hora, the medieval town that surrounds the monastery on the hill, the confidence that goes hand in hand with material ease is palpable. Hora's whitewashed stone houses were built by merchants and captains in the days when the island was a tax-free haven under the monastery's protection. The solidity of these homes, their fine artisanship and their sweeping views all combine to dispel shadowy thoughts about worldly impermanence.

Wealthy outsiders prop up Hora's well-mannered facade: many of its houses are owned by North Americans and Europeans who employ Greeks as housekeepers, or as house-sitters during the winter months. These local servants, too, had been infected by cleaning fever. They flung open doors and windows and hung rugs over balconies, affording me glimpses into homes that had the immaculate appearance of a Vermeer interior.

Patmos is more self-possessed, more stylish than Thira, but its means of survival are similar: here, too, the farmers have gradually been replaced by hotel-keepers, cafe owners and

67

restaurateurs; only the monks have preserved a traditional way of life. But while Thira is visibly the result of an apocalyptic upheaval, on Patmos the dark thread of apocalypse is invisible. The contrast between its bourgeois veneer and the horror that has compelled its religious life is extreme.[‡]

><

Patmos is beautiful, but St John is believed to have turned his back on mere appearances when he wrote his mysterious book. According to tradition, he dictated Revelations to his scribe while lying in a small, dark cave. Since St John's day, this secret place on the hillside below Hora has been elaborately delineated: the Monastery of the Cave of the Apocalypse has been built around it, and a small forest of cypress and pine trees planted on its perimeter.

A human thicket of tourists stood among these trees and blocked my way to the entrance of the cave. They wore holiday clothes: mini-skirts, shorts, swimming costumes. Men and women laughed uproariously as they wrapped towels around their legs or climbed into baggy skirts and trousers provided by the monks, too much flesh being frowned upon in the holy place.

By the time I made my way past them, the cave was so crammed with sightseers – listening to radios, brandishing cameras, discussing what they wanted to eat for lunch – that a sense of awe or mystery stood little chance. The crush was as disorienting, and as spiritually resonant, as a crowded shopping mall.

The cave had been converted into a chapel. Indentations in the rock, where St John is said to have rested his head and hand, had been edged in silver; the protruding stone ledge where his scribe is believed to have stood writing was draped in gold-embroidered cloth. At least thirty people had squeezed into the tiny space to peer at the three-pronged crack that is said to have appeared when the Lord spoke the words: "I am Alpha and Omega, the first and the last . . . What thou seest, write in a book."

Walking down a stone corridor on the way out of the monastery, I impulsively opened a heavy, wooden door. Behind it, a circle of middle-aged matrons were cheerfully polishing gold and silver – more cleaning for the anniversary. I fought an impulse to pick up a cloth and join them. These women belonged to this place; they knew what they were doing there. I apologised for intruding, but they smiled and assured me I hadn't disturbed them.

Outside, another busload of tourists was approaching. I jumped into a taxi that took me to the Monastery of St John the Theologian at the top of the hill. From here, Patmos was laid out like a book. I could trace the fluid line of its bays and inlets, as well as the peaks beyond: Ikaria, Samos and the archipelago of dots that punctuated the stretch of water between them. It was an orderly and tranquil sight. Beauty endowed the scene with the appearance of rightness: all the elements of the world – the farms, the houses, the fishing boats, the rocky peaks fringed by the sea – looked fixed and perfect. And yet it is speculated that this is the very view which inspired St John to write: 'And the heaven departed as a scroll when it is rolled together; and every mountain and island were moved out of their places' (Revelations 6:14).

My reverie was interrupted by the arrival of more bus tours, and the monastery was soon infected by the now familiar mood of manic, purposeless haste. I dashed from room to room, my eyes flitting over the precious icons and scrolls without taking them in.

I wanted to talk to a monk about the Apocalypse celebration, and put my request to a man in civilian clothes who was officiating at the monastery. He told me to go read a book: a standard Greek response to interview requests at historic sites. I persisted until he fetched a slender young monk, Father Simeon, who politely heard me out and told me to return the next day for a reply.

Father Simeon's thinness gave him the elongated, ethereal look of a Byzantine icon. As we talked, he kept his eyes firmly fixed on the wall behind my shoulder in what I took to be a mannered otherworldliness. He told me that whether or not we would be able to speak at greater length was out of my hands and up to God; in the meantime, he recommended prayer.

I bit back a smile but the monk saw it. He looked straight at me for the first time. "Do you pray?"

"Yes."

"Good. Pray for this." As he walked away, my smile returned against my will. In all my years as a journalist no-one had ever suggested that I pray for an interview.

Early the next morning I returned to the monastery as arranged. The crowds had not yet arrived. The walls had been freshly whitewashed and the quadrangle hung with golden banners emblazoned with the two-headed eagle of Byzantium. A vacuum cleaner lay coiled in a corner.

Father Simeon was showing the monastery's icon collection to a Greek family; he motioned me to join them. I soon realised that the Father's remote manner was deceptive: for him, Byzantine art was a deeply felt passion. We lingered before images I had barely noticed the previous day; the paintings glowed like jewels. Father Simeon remarked that the art of Greek Orthodoxy glows with an inner light, and that "foreigners don't easily enter into the spirit of it."

A common complaint about Byzantine art is that the images are static and monotonous. But on this morning it seemed to me that the icons were animated by such gravity and compassion that a sense of movement was unnecessary. In a thirteenth-century icon of the Virgin and Child, for instance, the portrait of the Virgin was long, flat and, on the face of it, unlovely; the Christ child was stiff and small like a doll. But none of this mattered. The images were unlocked – as real faces are – by looking into their eyes. The figures floated on gold, my eye was drawn into their gaze and, once caught, had little choice but to contemplate the emotion concentrated there.

When he had finished his duties as a guide, Father Simeon agreed to talk to me. He was a shy, quiet man. He had come to Patmos because of his lifelong fascination with the Apocalypse. The Book of Revelation could of course be read on a symbolic level, but Orthodoxy also took the prophecy literally: an Apocalypse would come, a time of terrible judgment would arrive.

He described tourism on Patmos as tragic. He was not talking about its impact on island life, but about the effects of direction-less pleasure-seeking on the tourists themselves. Revelations warns of the fate that awaits hedonists, the faithless and the ignorant.

"The joy and beauty that can be found in the world is fleeting," said Father Simeon. "In truth, life means suffering. Faith, faith is the key: the key to our understanding and to our salvation." His words – familiar, ritualistic – brought me back to the atmosphere surrounding the icons.

It turned out that Father Simeon was also an icon painter, working in the Byzantine style. And here, perhaps, lay the difficulty, the gap, between the words he spoke and the faith from which they sprang. Today's icon painters are, essentially, copyists; and a copy, no matter how skilful, re-creates the appearance of an original, but not the vision that created it. If anything, the reverse is true: visual repetition has worked to reduce the images of the Byzantine masters to a kind of holy shorthand. In the same way, although the monk knew what he loved about his faith, he was only able to speak about it with old, worn-out words. His passion could not penetrate his language.

><

The restaurant kitchen was brimming with late-summer and autumn fare: *yemista*, tomatoes stuffed with seasoned rice; *briam*, vegetable stew with eggplant; lima beans baked with tomatoes and garlic; fresh, boiled beetroot with *skordalya*, garlic sauce. I over-ordered again; it had become a bad habit on Patmos. The restaurants here were the best I had seen on the islands. In the patisseries, pyramids of *kourambyedes*, Greek shortbreads dusted with icing sugar and stuffed with almonds and walnuts, were arranged next to trays of croissants and crisp baguettes. Store-bought *kourambyedes* are usually a disappointment; on Patmos they became a daily addiction.

As I tucked into my dinner, the chef came out and seated himself at the next table. He was a jolly, portly man, but his vitality drained from him as he sat down to his own supper. Hunching dully over his food, he ate straight from a saucepan filled with a mush of milk, bread, coffee and sugar; there was a side dish of olives and feta. He caught me staring at this dismal scene and spread out his hands as if to say, "What am I to do?" He reminded me of my father, who ran a restaurant of his own for thirty years. He would come home around midnight and my mother would make him a cheese or cold meat sandwich; it was often his only meal of the day. I grew up witnessing a daily parable about the dangers of excess and the limited pleasures of the flesh.

The next morning I went up to Hora to see if I could talk to a restaurateur whose name had been given to me in Australia. Mr Poulos was reputedly a wonderful fellow: an excellent raconteur and host, a kindly man and a good businessman. He appeared to lead a charmed life. His summers were spent running what some said was the best restaurant in the Aegean, while in the winter he worked as the front man in one of the most famous restaurants in New York.

His Patmos restaurant was in an inconspicuous stone house, tucked away in a side street; I found it by following the bay leaf and tomato smells that spilled into the nearby lanes. The door was opened by a grey-haired woman, dressed entirely in black. I asked for Mr Poulos and she told me he was her husband and would be home soon; then she invited me in. She spoke English with an accent that was part Greek, part New York.

As we walked down the corridor, her grown-up daughter came down the stairs. The girl looked weary and preoccupied. "Where are you going, my dear?" asked her mother.

"To Skala. Maybe for a swim."

Mrs Poulos deftly motioned her daughter over to the stove and showed her a saucepan with a brown stew in it. "This is the meal I made for you. When you're ready, come home and eat it." The daughter, seeing that her mother was concerned for her, kissed her on the cheek, smiled at the stew, and left.

Mrs Poulos led me into the kitchen, where an elegant blonde woman sat at the table, spreading cheese on biscuits with manicured hands. Anne was visiting from upstate New York. She looked a most unlikely friend for Mrs Poulos, and yet there was clearly a strong bond between them. Mrs Poulos began plying us with coffee and homemade *kourambyedes* as Anne made small talk about Australia. I tried to talk to Mrs Poulos about her restaurant but she was unwilling to engage directly with me and began rummaging in drawers for magazine articles about the place.

Then Mr Poulos came in with some shopping. To my surprise, he was a jowly, slow-moving man, weighed down by a heaviness that was not simply caused by the bags he was carrying. He was much older than I had expected, but then again so was his wife. When she introduced me, Mr Poulos sat down at the opposite end of the kitchen, turned his back to us and said: "I don't give interviews." It was impossible to be offended by his blunt refusal, as the morning's activities had obviously sapped him of the little energy he had.

I probably should have left then. But the smells in the restaurant kitchen were familiar, and the half-Greek, half-American inflections of Mr and Mrs Poulos reminded me of the kitchen-table conversations of my own family. Despite themselves, these people had given me the momentary illusion of being at home.

Mrs Poulos automatically smoothed over the awkwardness of her husband's words. She smiled at me and began to tell me about herself. Her mother had died when she was a baby, so although she had been born in New York she had been raised by relatives on Patmos. The restaurant's menu featured the recipes she had learned while she was growing up, along with some French and

Italian dishes that her husband prepared; Greeks were disappointed if all the dishes were local.

Their clientele came from all over the world; in the season, Hora was an international city. What did it matter if Europeans owned Hora's fine houses? Greeks could not afford to restore all of them, and the French and the Germans, the Swiss and the Italians who had purchased property there – they were all good people. She spoke briskly, as though by rote. Now she paused: was that enough? I thanked her and quickly browsed through the magazine article she had finally located. It quoted *two* Mr Pouloses. I turned to Mrs Poulos, who was watching me patiently: Where was the other Mr Poulos?

"My son is dead," said Mrs Poulos. "He died last year."

I took in the mother in black, the father's unaffected weariness, the blonde woman at the table and remembered the daughter's listlessness. All the puzzle's pieces were joined, or so it seemed, by this single loss.

Mrs Poulos touched me on the arm, brushing away apologies. "Let me show you around the restaurant." We went into the dining room, where she showed me the stylish menu and talked about the embroidery samplers and family photographs on the walls. They were mementoes from her mother, her grandmother and her great-grandmother; her family had lived in the house for seven generations. The eyes of the women in the photographs held the same expression as the kind, grave eyes of Mrs Poulos. I pointed out the family resemblance and she said yes, everybody noticed it. The family had drawn her back to this place, and now they were enduring together.

><

Before I left Father Simeon, he had suggested I contact Father Antipas. He'd written down the telephone number and told me that his fellow monk could be found at the Loukakia every afternoon. Everybody knew the Loukakia: it was a spiritual retreat on the beach outside Skala.

Patmos is dotted with spiritual retreats as other islands are dotted with cocktail bars, for even though the island is small, its geography makes isolation possible. The coastline is indented with secluded inlets and even smaller islands crowd the shores, making it an ideal haven for solitary ascetics. Theologos, the man who owned my hotel, told me that when he was a child, a hermit had made his home on the tiny white island that I could see from my balcony. The monk had lived among the stones and the birds' nests. Theologos mimicked how a hermit walks if he has been on a rocky island for too long, lifting his feet in high, exaggerated steps so as not to trip over imaginary stones.

Craggy Patmos evokes the contradictory impressions of intimacy and lonely wilderness: the land is full of stones, fresh water is scarce, the villages are isolated, and nearly every mountain crest has a view of the sea and the islands beyond. Yet all these elements somehow combine into a harmonious whole. Before coming to the island, I had been intrigued by the idea that some special quality inherent in its atmosphere or geography had manifested itself in St John's vision. But once there I forgot about the gloom or awe I had expected and instead felt gratitude for the island's beauty. It was more than enough.

On the day I was to meet Father Antipas I lunched on a crowded beach, surrounded by topless Germans who ignored the signs asking them to keep their clothes on because Patmos was holy. Everybody looked content: the grandmothers, the children, the hearty young men, the glamorous girls in string bikinis. I swam, ate brown bread, olives, cheese and fresh tomatoes, and then swam again. The water was still and warm. My body loosened up and the Apocalypse slipped away. I tried to remember the dark fascination it had once held for me, but I could no longer connect with it – or even remember why I had ever wanted to. I was floating in the water, filled to overflowing with temporal happiness.

The Loukakia was easy to find; it was built to look like a castle, its style echoing the Monastery of St John the Theologian. Here, too, the monks were cleaning up a storm in preparation for the arrival of the Serbian Patriarch, who was due the next day. A row of icons lined the yard and a monk was carefully dusting their frames with a cloth.

Father Antipas was surprisingly young and fresh-faced, with a direct and intelligent countenance. His parents had returned to Patmos from Sydney when he was very young; he had attended Sunday services in the Cave of the Apocalypse, where he had received his calling at the age of six. From that time he had known for certain that Christ was the only truth. "I know this is hard to believe," he said. "I can't understand it myself, that a boy could understand the falseness of the world."

His enlightenment in the cave animated him still. The world was wrong-headed, he believed; the earth was sick. Socialism had failed and capitalism was not the answer. Brakes had to be applied to what was called progress: industry, car production, pollution. Asked about development in his own region, he said he did not believe that tourism, of itself, was evil: the evil occurred when it took place in a cultural vacuum, when the local people allowed themselves to be indiscriminately swamped by outside influences.

The Father's faith was closely bound to his patriotism.

Greece, he believed, was turning away from its destiny, with catastrophic results for the nation and for the world. Greeks needed to re-examine their heritage, to return to their classical and Byzantine roots – two unique civilisations that only the Greek mind could have produced. The way forward was impossible without their influence, but a young, educated Greek today was likely to be more familiar with Marxist theory than with his country's past. Modern Greeks were attempting to find nourishment in cultures that had less intrinsic value than their own. He believed that the result of the country's malaise could be seen in the continuous, losing battle over borders: Cyprus, Asia Minor, Constantinople, Northern Epiros. All had once been Greek lands; all were now lost.

Father Antipas was doing what he could at the Loukakia. Building on land he had inherited from his family, he had created a quiet place where men who were interested in the Church could experience the monastic life. So far, the retreat had been responsible for five souls entering the Church.

A young monk interrupted us with a question about the preparations for the Serbian Patriarch; the brothers were clearly frantic about the amount of work still left to do. It was time for me to leave. As I walked down the drive I heard Father Antipas call out more instructions: "And don't forget to wash the windowsills."

><

In Skala the party atmosphere was infectious. The port was filling up with grand yachts sailing in for the anniversary show. Nobody was sure exactly who was arriving but the rumours were rife: the Greek cabinet was coming and maybe a few generals, some shipping millionaires perhaps, or the Clintons and the Gores. Even the aristocracy of Hora had missed out on seats to the main events, and it was this fact that convinced me it would be crazy to stay. I would certainly be reduced to watching the celebrations on television, just like everybody else.

On my last morning, hacks from central casting took over the hotel dining room. They carried mobile phones, cameras, fatigue jackets and an air of anxious self-importance. I unintentionally sent a Brazilian photographer scurrying up the road to Hora by mentioning that a television crew was recording vox pops on Armageddon at the Monastery of St John. (I had returned there for one last look at the icons, realising that these enigmatic images somehow held the key to what I had hoped to find on the island, and wanting to seal them in my memory before I left.)

Golden Byzantine flags were strung around the port and the last piece of scaffolding had been removed from the post office. A crowd had gathered to watch a marching band all dressed in white with brass knobs on their safari hats. The band, which would have looked at home on the set of *Casablanca*, was rehearsing a welcome for the VIPs who were expected later that day – although not even the journalists could say for certain who they would be.

Among the sightseers was Pano, my sceptical companion from the ferry, loaded down with bottles of cola for his mates. He grinned a greeting. "We did our work, we bought our icons, and now we're going," he said.

Icons? Why?

"For the wife, you know." He paused. "And, well, at bottom, I too believe that something is up there, something exists. What do you say?"

We looked at the bustling activity all around us – the band, the yachts, the journalists, the scurrying waiters. All of them, believers and unbelievers alike, were propelled by a ritual obeisance to an invisible life. Pano beamed a curious, ironic smile. Then he picked up his bottles of cola and walked away in the sunshine, to the rousing accompaniment of the Apocalypse birthday band.

* Tony's dream brought two passages from the Book of Revelation to mind. One is the description of the Four Horsemen of the Apocalypse: 'And power was given unto them over the fourth part of the earth, to kill with the sword, and with hunger, and with death, and with the beasts of the earth' (Revelations 6:8).

  The other is from Revelations 9:6: 'And in those days shall men seek death, and shall not find it; and shall desire to die, and death shall flee from them'.

† The name Christodoulos – it means Christ's worker – is still popular on Patmos, as is the name Theologos (literally, the Word of God), the epithet the Orthodox Church attaches to St John.

‡ St John lived through the time of Nero's suicide, the burning of Rome and the plague that followed, the fall of Jerusalem and the eruption of Vesuvius (the last two events had been linked to the prophecy of an ancient oracle). He filled the Book of Revelation with phenomena

resembling the aftermath of a mighty volcanic blast: earthquakes, a hail of stones and black clouds so dense that they darkened the sun. Ashes from Vesuvius blew as far east as Egypt and Syria, and we see echoes of the disaster in Revelations.

Since St John's time, seismological disturbances on Thira have been linked to God's displeasure. The eighth-century chronicler Theophanes described how 'steam as a fiery furnace bubbled up from the depths of the sea between the islands of Thira and Thirasia . . . Large pumice stones were spewed out all over Asia Minor, Lesbos . . . and towards those parts of Macedonia that overlook the sea'. This eruption was considered particularly significant, as it coincided with a theological dispute, the Iconoclastic Controversy, which was then rocking the Byzantine world.

CHAPTER FOUR

THE ISLAND OF DREAMS

T HE *GOLDEN VERGINA* was a big, shabby, old ferry moored at the far end of the port of Samos. It was Sunday afternoon. I had been sitting alone on the boat for hours, waiting to leave for Ikaria. I had arrived early, but there appeared to be some delay and nobody was around to ask what the problem was. So I sat in the sun, doing nothing in particular.

Time was suspended. The normally busy port was empty and the afternoon hush felt as if it would never end. All the activities that fill the toiling world had ceased: all conversation, exercise, drudgery, schemes for self-improvement, projects taken up to divert oneself from life's melancholy undertow, acts of daring, of folly or sexual necessity.

That time alone with nothing to do was a great and unexpected blessing: it had been months, maybe years, since I had last had such a stretch of unmarked time before me. Greece is full of people who are unashamedly idle. Men and women will pull up a chair on the street outside their house and simply sit: maybe something interesting will happen. Outside the cities and off the tourist trail, people still stop to ask you questions; because you are there, and therefore a diversion, but also because it is a deep-seated reflex, particularly among older people, to reach out to strangers. Maybe they will like you, maybe you will connect; there is no shame attached to having nothing to do, and to exposing your interest in, and perhaps your liking for, an unknown soul.

On the *Golden Vergina* that lazy afternoon I couldn't help but recall – and recoil at – the busyness that had come to mark my life, and the isolation that came with it, the sense it gave that I had lost control, lost what was valuable in life.

An unexpected change to the inter-island timetables had forced me to stay on Samos for five days before leaving for Lesbos, where I had arranged to meet some friends from Australia (friends I had barely seen for two years at home due to lack of time). The hydrofoil service that normally connects the two islands had suddenly stopped running, for reasons which were never adequately explained.

It goes without saying that a traveller's impressions are subjective: someone hates Paris because that was where they made the break with their best friend, but Idaho is thrilling because it cured them of eczema. Before I had left for Greece, a friend had taken me aside to warn me of the dangers of the search for 'realness'. It was folly, she'd said, to talk about tourism making places 'unreal'. You could lament its effects, but what existed *was* real, a tourism-altered world was reality now. On Samos, tourism meant that the island had no particularity that I could discern, no edge of its own. The island was fat, green and prosperous, as comfortable as the suburbs. The pastel awnings on the cafes, the menus in three languages, the shops selling plaster reproductions of Botticelli's Venus – all of this dulled the experience of being there.

And so I decided to escape to Ikaria, about which I knew nothing. To a surprising degree, the Greek islands operate as separate and distinct worlds. Islands are natural fortresses; their walls are the sea. Although only a short ferry ride away, Samos was supremely indifferent to the Apocalypse celebrations on Patmos. Once I had put Patmos behind me, it no longer felt necessary to be continually on the watch for signs of imminent doom. And thus I hoped that Ikaria, likewise, would be different from Samos. I was not disappointed.

><

The *Golden Vergina* was heading for Piraeus. Only a few earnest northern European backpackers disembarked with me at Evdilos, Ikaria's secondary port. We straggled off the ferry, along with a young black calf on the back of a truck; farmers were evidently still working the island. Most of the backpackers jumped into cabs waiting to take them to Armenistis, a nearby beach resort. I didn't want to visit another resort and so found myself, to my surprise, walking alone along a small, unlit harbour.

Summer had officially ended that day, daylight saving was over (this was the reason the ferry had been delayed), and although it was not late, the sky was already dark and full of stars. Many hotels and rooms for rent had closed for the season, but I eventually found a clean, old-fashioned room near the sea, with linoleum on the floors and a bathroom down the hall.

Only one taverna was open: a rough, concrete-floored place serving souvlakia, salad and tzatziki on paper tablecloths. Evdilos was the first truly quiet town I had seen on the islands. The rusticity of the place reminded me of my father's village in the Peloponnese. The liveliest spot in town was outside the *periptero*, or kiosk, where newspapers, cigarettes, cold drinks and the like were sold. It was well lit and the chain-smoking owner was doing a brisk trade in gossipy small talk.

After my meal there was nowhere to go but my room. I lay in bed listening to the wind roaring down from the mountains, felt a sharp pang of loneliness and fell asleep at nine o'clock.

The next morning I woke early. Aromas from the bakery next door wafted into my room and I breakfasted on two warm *koulourya*: crispy, ring-shaped, sesame-covered rolls. A Norwegian couple were the only other people stirring at the little U-shaped harbour; like me, they planned to take the early bus to the island's capital of Agios Kirykos. I left my bag at the bus stop and walked around the harbour. Two giant cement-block reefs had been dumped in the water, an ugly measure designed to promote the breeding of fish. The reefs gave Evdilos a perverse appeal: here was a place where fish were more important than the aesthetics required by tourism.

The road connecting Evdilos and Agios Kirykos was one of the few sealed roads on Ikaria; it followed the deeply fissured coast before crossing the mountain range that rose in the centre of the island. The two-hour bus ride was a shock: I was utterly unprepared for Ikaria. It was a jungle in the middle of the Aegean.

Savage, extreme, rude, cruel, not to trust – the line in Shakes-peare's sonnet about lust leapt to mind. His words described a loss of control that matched the intense, luxuriant forest and the steep mountains unfolding outside the bus window. The island bore no resemblance to the stony, sun-flooded lands of Apollo that dot the Aegean. Ikaria was more akin to the remote moun-tains of Arcadia, magically ripped from the heart of the Peloponnese and dumped into the sea. In myth, the island was the birthplace of Dionysos. This made imaginative sense: the ancients may well have made a link between the unfettered lushness of the topography and the Dionysiac-affected psyche.

Our route veered erratically past the shaggy, tangled growth of the mountains. For the first part of our journey, most of the road was overshadowed by a dense confusion of olives, figs, plane trees and oaks. But once we reached the mountaintop the sun flooded in, exposing great skulls of bare rock. The bus filled with warmth and, on our descent, the wind dropped. The eastern side of the island still bore the scars of bushfires from a previous season; we drove past a mighty, charred oak, its blackened leaves still clinging to the branches, as though preserved in tar.

Agios Kirykos was bigger than Evdilos, but it still retained the atmosphere of a country backwater. There were no boutiques or flash hotels, just a line of cafes on the waterfront. I visited the ferry office, and then tried to plan my next move over a coffee. The news was bad. It was Monday morning, and I had to be back at Samos on Wednesday to make the connection to Lesbos. But the next ferry to Samos didn't leave until Wednesday at 2 am; my only other option was to catch the bi-weekly hydrofoil leaving that afternoon.

My true frustration, however, lay not with the ferry timetables but with myself. Ikaria – the wild island that I had dreamed of exploring – was a nut I could not crack. Most of it was inaccessible by public transport. If, for instance, I wanted to visit the tenth-century castle of Nikarias in the mountains or the temple of Artemis at Nas, I needed to hire a car. But Ikaria's twisting mountain roads were narrow and unsealed, and my fear of driving was, alas, a demon I had not completely conquered.

I sipped my coffee, not knowing what to do. At the next table, a beautiful blonde German girl and two self-consciously handsome Greek men were drinking beer as an accompaniment to the eggs and cigarettes that made up their breakfast. They sat inertly, their conversation desultory and disconnected. Judging from the number of soiled plates and glasses on their table, they had been sitting there for hours. One of the men wore his shirt unbuttoned and had an incongruously feminine gold bangle on his wrist; periodically he would stand and circle around the other two, rubbing his hand slowly over his chest in a dreamlike, narcissistic dance.

A northern European family sat close by. A toddler ran up to his mother and slapped her. With a cool economy of movement, she pushed him to the ground and twisted his hand behind his back. Neither mother or son spoke, and the father and daughter who were also at the table paid scant attention. The boy walked over to another table, where he pulled his T-shirt over his head as his mother returned to her breakfast.

A group of local teenagers sat at a third table. A woman in her thirties approached them with a video camera and said: "I want to find out what the young people are thinking." Her pronouncement set off a wave of self-consciousness among the group, who responded by affecting indifference, even contempt. The woman pointed the camera at one of the boys, who then lifted his arm towards his girlfriend's face as if to strike her. The girlfriend was gravely handsome, with a natural dignity, and she looked coldly at the boy as the woman lowered her camera. "Never!" admonished the woman. "Never, never, not even in jest."

Still affected by the morning's shadow-shrouded bus ride, I had the surreal thought that the dark spirits of the forest had somehow clothed themselves in flesh and travelled to the waterfront. I forced myself to stop staring and pulled out my journal. The familiar act of writing soon had the desired effect of providing emotional detachment; by the time I put my pen down, the tables were empty and I had decided to visit the *eparchos*, or mayor of the province.

Mr Tripodis was a broad-faced, avuncular fellow who agreed to see me immediately. He shared his office with Niko, a council employee, and Grigori, a straight-backed old man who sat in a chair at the back of the room. As Mr Tripodis talked about the excellence of Ikaria and all who lived there, Grigori silently played with his worry beads, or *komboloi*. From his deliberate, slow movements and his shabby, well-pressed clothes, but mostly from a remote, otherworldly look in his eyes, I guessed that he had spent most of his life in the mountains. On the office walls were black-and-white photographs of mustachioed, triumphant men with straps of ammunition crossed over their chests. I could imagine Grigori looking like those men in his youth, and I asked Mr Tripodis who they were.

"Yes, yes, that's it!" cried the old man with sudden vigour. "That's what you should be talking about!"

The mayor appeared to notice him for the first time. "My friend," he said, "later we will both sit and talk for a long time, but not now," and he gestured towards me. The old man, appeased by this courtesy, rose slowly, bowed and left.

Mr Tripodis said the photographs were taken in July 1912,

when Ikaria became the first northern Aegean island to free itself from Turkish rule. The island did not become part of Greece until October that year; in the interim it was a separate country, with its own laws and constitution.

Just then another council employee ran into the room in a state of high excitement. He threw a fax on the table and shouted that he had had enough, that these faxes from Athens were more than he could bear. No-one looked surprised, and the mayor left the office to deal with the crisis. This left me alone with Niko.

"What's so funny?" he asked.

"Nothing. I just like it here."

He was an intelligent, softly spoken fellow. He regarded me for a moment then pointed to a map of Ikaria on the wall.

"This is a most remarkable place," he said. "Do you know that for 300 years, during the time of the pirates, all the people on the island hid in a village that is surrounded by large rocks?" He pointed to a village in the centre of the map. "Here they were invisible from the sea. They lived a socialist kind of life: they ate together, they farmed together, there were no landlords and they had to live according to fair and just principles because they couldn't survive any other way. The village still exists; you should go there."

Niko went on to tell me that he and his wife, Eleni, farmed land at a village near the coast; they rented a flat in town during the week and went to the farm every weekend. As if on cue, Eleni walked into the office with Mr Tripodis. They were obviously friends; she was kissing the mayor on the head, to his delight and confusion. We were introduced and she immediately began asking me about my father's village and the conditions of women there.

"I know about the Peloponnese," she said, before I had

formulated my answer. "They are under the thumb," and she demonstrated the expression by making a gesture with her hand. "But the women here are like nowhere else in Greece. They were left alone for so many years while their men went to sea that they took charge of their farms. Go to a village *kafeneion* here and you will see that they are full of women; and they will be drinking beer too, not just lemonade. Would you like to see that? Niko and I will show you around Ikaria if you like. You could stay with us on our farm."

I asked Eleni how she found living in a small, isolated community. "It's all right if you don't have a problem with yourself," she replied.

Eleni was small and feisty, and as she spoke, she crossed the room to stand next to Niko. Suddenly she put her arms around his belly and laughed: "Aren't we well matched? I'm so small and he's so big and fat." I was bowled over. Liking someone at first sight is a condition almost as disorienting as its better known cousin. My confusion must have been apparent because Eleni repeated her invitation: "If you would like to visit us, you will be welcome, but you must give us some notice first."

I left the mayor's office frustrated because I could not take up Eleni and Nick's offer of friendship: bad timing, lack of time, the pressures of time. A cab drove by; I took it to the nearby town of Therma, to see its famous radioactive springs. I was still preoccupied with Niko and Eleni, but the driver, Nikiphoros, soon commanded all my attention. He was a philosopher in a white boiler suit, and was holding forth about the impact of the airport that was due to open in time for the following season: "We don't want many tourists here and let me tell you why. Now when you stop my taxi, I see you, as a person, Katerina. I ask you about Katerina, and then you ask about me: we meet in a good, human way. But if many tourists come, forget it. I won't see you as a person any more. All I will think about is how much money you have in your wallet."

Therma was a modest town where the predominantly elderly visitors walked the streets in bathrobes with towels on their heads. The springs themselves were scattered around at various sites; their different waters were used for different ailments – arthritis, rheumatism, skin complaints, even infertility. The spa facilities looked worn and in need of repair. I was not tempted to try them, so Nikiphoros drove me back to the waterfront cafe I'd had coffee at that morning.

The cafe's tables were shaded by trees and overlooked the dazzling aquamarine waters of the harbour. In the distance, the cone-shaped silhouettes of the Fourni Islands were emerging from the midday heat haze. I sat down and buried my head in my journal again, when suddenly a voice said: "So what are you going to do?"

Niko stood before me, smiling ironically. I explained the stupid mess of the ferry timetables and my appointment in Lesbos.

"I'd like to drive you around," he said, "but I can't just drop everything."

"Also, you don't know me."

"I understand the person," he said, and then he sat with me and ordered two beers and a plate of *mezedes* for our lunch.

Winter was the best season, anyway, Niko told me. That was when I should return. Then all the tourists and the summer residents would have left, and with only the committed, the true Ikarians remaining, the community was more closely bound together. And in the cold weather, the island was more beautiful; waterfalls tumbled from the mountaintops.

Niko was not from Ikaria; his people came from the Ionian island of Lefkada. He and Eleni had met in Athens and married there. He grimaced when he spoke of Athens: its traffic, its noise, the little cement boxes in which one was forced to live.

Now he spent every weekend in an old house without electricity, telephone or running water. His fellow villagers had 'baptised' him: they'd made him an honorary Ikarian by dousing him with water from a clay pot. The decision to return to the village – to the past – was not that unusual, he said. People were slowly going back to the country ways. Life in the cities was becoming untenable. The old ways were harder, but there was health and poetry in them; they fed the soul. An example: elderly Ikarians still walked great distances – if they tended goats they walked maybe thirty kilometres a day – and they were as strong as cypress trees. In the old days, people had walked all over the island. If their walks took more than a day, they spent the night in cells maintained by the island's priests; the cells still existed.

Ikaria was a place like no other, according to Niko. Had I noticed the singsong way in which the old people spoke? It was ancient Greek. As recently as this century an Ikarian community had still celebrated the rite of the wind, as they had in ancient times; the practice was stopped when a village priest threatened to excommunicate them.

With deftness, with quiet charm, with grave authority, Niko wove a spell. He spoke about Ikaria as though it were a magical world – a secret preserver of what was good in life. Longing stirred in me. Niko had unwittingly described the place I had secretly hoped for; he had helped me understand why it was that I had come to the Aegean.

I looked up and smiled, realising that all this would remain unsaid. Niko asked me about life in Australia, and I related a more prosaic story: the long hours people worked (Niko, as a public servant, finished work at two in the afternoon); the dearth of community life; the endemic lack of time and the empty belief that relentless activity equalled fulfilment.

"So it's true what they say then?"

"What do they say?"

"That Greeks are the only people left in the world who know how to enjoy life."

Niko decided to order another beer from the bar, and while he did so, I eavesdropped on an elderly couple at the next table. They were ordering coffee and giving the waiter meticulous instructions about the proportion of sugar to coffee they required. The waiter listened attentively; he was in no hurry.

When Niko returned with his drink, he leant forward suddenly and said, sharply: "Decide!"

"Decide what?"

"Where will you live? You're a Greek – how can you live the life you have been living?"

I didn't know how to answer, and when I boarded the hydro-foil soon after, I was still trying to work it out. I regretted that abrupt ending to a conversation and a friendship. And I regretted that I had not been able to say: show me that all you have told me is true about Ikaria.

Twilight fell. The sky, the sea and the land were darkening, changing from pink and mauve to purple and blue. We were approaching the Fourni Islands. Again, I felt that I had no choice: I set my regrets aside, leant towards the open door, and took in the beauty of the fleeting view.

CHAPTER FIVE

SAPPHO'S ISLAND

IN A SQUARE near the beach at Skala Eresou stands a small white bust of the philosopher Theophrastus. He has a good view. The silver beach is long and sandy; its air of lonely wildness fulfils even an Australian's exacting standards of what a good beach should be. At one end of the beach is a bare, rocky hill, the acropolis of Ancient Eresos. In the long grass that skirts the hill you can find remnants of stone walls, built before the time of Homer. Strong and perfect still, they stand impassively in the goat paddocks, surrounded by thistles and thorny oak trees.

Theophrastus was born at Eresos in 372 BC, more than a thousand years after the walls were built. Now considered a minor philosopher, he was well known, even revered, in his day.

He taught and wrote in Athens just after its glory days, in the years when the Macedonians ruled Greece, and while Alexander was in the east conquering the Persians and becoming Great.

The teacher of Alexander's youth was the philosopher Aristotle. When Theophrastus left Lesbos, he went to Athens and also studied with the mighty philosopher. Theophrastus was known as Tyrtamos then, but he so impressed Aristotle with the beauty of his writing that Aristotle gave him a new name: Theophrastus means divine speaker. The young philosopher went on to succeed Aristotle as the head of his Athenian academy and inherited his library. He wrote about volcanoes, the weather, stones, plants, wine, smells and animal behaviour. But his longest surviving work is not philosophical or scientific: *The Characters* is a brief collection of sketches describing the range of scurrilous and ridiculous men then found on the streets of Athens. Each sketch begins with a definition, a display of precision and wit. (Of the Superstitious Man, for example, Theophrastus writes: 'Ah yes, superstition: it would appear to be cowardice in the face of the supernatural'.) The book is said to have been a great influence on the comic playwright Menander, one of Theophrastus's pupils, but it is chiefly remembered because it brings the scoundrels of his age so vividly to life. Pithy and resonant, it can still make you laugh out loud.

It was Theophrastus's fate to have been born in the same town as the poet Sappho, who came into the world two and a half centuries before him, in 610 BC. In Theophrastus's time, Sappho was so highly esteemed that Plato – who also taught Theophrastus – dubbed her 'the tenth muse'. She still has many followers. During the warm months, women from around the world make the long pilgrimage to the beach at Skala Eresou to honour her. But in the square – the place where logic and sentiment dictate that they should find a stone or plaque to Sappho – Theophrastus's bald head looks out instead. Not many visitors have heard of the philosopher and so he is mostly ignored; the women have come to give a garland to Sappho. Her statue, however, is a two-and-a-half-hour drive away, at the edge of the harbour in Mytilini, the capital of Lesbos and the city where the poet spent most of her life.

Skala Eresou is peaceful, out of the way. Tourism transforms it for a few months each year, but a sense of its winter quietness never completely leaves the town. Sappho's fame is responsible for many of the tourists who journey to its silver-grey beach, but I cannot remember even a sign in Skala Eresou that mentions her. A hotel-keeper explained the omission: the townspeople had nothing against the immortal poet – it was the pilgrims they objected to. The hotel-keeper was a portly, timid man. When he mentioned the women, he dropped his voice, squirming a little. The women were so overtly, so demonstratively *lèsbian*. They held hands and kissed on the beach. They shaved their heads. Sometimes they fought among themselves. It was distasteful, the town disapproved. If I intended to write about Skala Eresou, perhaps it would be best not to mention Sappho: it would only encourage the women.

At this, another resident, a professional man, nodded in agreement. A great deal could be written about the area without mentioning Sappho, he said. Besides, he believed that the lesbian pilgrimage to her birthplace was misguided, the result of an unfortunate historical misunderstanding. There was no evidence that Sappho was homosexual. The rumours about her sexuality began with Menander, but her contemporaries had been silent on the matter; satirists had enjoyed making ribald jokes about her and now, so many centuries later, Skala Eresou was suffering the consequences. As was all of Lesbos, indeed: its very name had become an allusion to Sappho's supposed sexual orientation, which was why so many Greeks called the island Mytilini.

Legend has it that Sappho killed herself for love by throwing herself off a cliff. She was short, dark and plain, and was known as the nightingale because her drab appearance belied the beauty of her song. Along with the female students in her school at Mytilini, she worshipped the goddess Aphrodite and honoured her divine gift, the sweet madness of love. Love was Sappho's religion and her muse; she believed it to be greater than war and the quest for power.

> *Some say thronging cavalry, some say foot soldiers,*
> *others call a fleet the most beautiful of sights*
> *the dark earth offers,*
> *but I say it's whatever you love best.*

Only a fraction of Sappho's work survives. Much of it was only discovered by accident, when members of the British Egypt Exploration Society scratching in the sands of Oxyrhyncus at the turn of the century came across papyrus fragments with lines of her poetry written on them.* Many of the Sapphic scraps are about the same length as a haiku, and they have the same delicacy and emotional immediacy:

> *Eros the Limb-loosener shakes me again –*
> *that sweet, bitter, impossible creature.*

> *Then love shook my heart like the wind that falls on*
> *oaks in the mountains.*

97

The moon has set
and the Pleiades; it is the middle of the night
and the hours go by
and I lie here alone.

Much of Sappho's writing celebrates the beauty of women and her love for the girls in her school. (One unattached line says simply: 'O beautiful, O graceful girl . . .') Talent rarely flourishes in a vacuum, and so it is believed that Sappho must have lived in a world in which women enjoyed a fuller, freer life than was allowed them in succeeding centuries. For how could Sappho alone have achieved the freedom of body and spirit that we can still glimpse in the broken mosaic of her work? So little is known about the other women of her time, however, that Sappho remains both a miracle and an enigma: the only female genius of the ancient world.

Meanwhile, it is a safe bet that Skala Eresou's unease with the Sapphists is a continuing source of amusement for the lonely bust of Theophrastus, providing a daily demonstration that in the late twentieth century human foibles have much the same texture as they did in his own time.

><

I arrived on Lesbos at 6 am and, out of habit, took a taxi to Mytilini's bus station. The cabbie, also acting out of habit, charged me an exorbitant amount for the short ride, causing me, in turn, to perform the now familiar ritual of cursing him soundly before slamming the door. A wispy-haired old lady, with one tooth left in her lower gum, watched me drag my suitcase to the seat beside her and, once I had done so, told me that the station would not be open for two hours. Then she asked brightly if I would walk to the other side of a nearby park to buy her a loaf of bread; she was particular about the kind of bread she wanted, describing it at some length.

This was not my first encounter with old Greek ladies of this type: Zen-like apparitions, they typically strike when their quarry is dazed and vulnerable. Once, when I was hitchhiking in Epiros, an old lady approached me as I clambered off the back of a utility truck; I had just endured a reckless downhill drive from the mountain village of Metsovo, during which the driver had taken hairpin bends from the wrong side of the road.

"*Herete*," said the crone, "would you be so kind as to give me some Nivea cream?" Shaken and covered with sawdust, I automatically opened my bag and gave her the cream. She thanked me and disappeared. Similarly, I now did as requested, eventually returning to the bus station with warm bread and *tiropites*, cheese pies, for our breakfast.

It was now October. I knew the warm weather would not last much longer, that my journey around the islands was almost at an end. I stared balefully at my luggage. My case was so heavy that its handle had broken after a few weeks, so heavy that I was tempted to stay in sub-standard places rather than lift it, so heavy that I inevitably arrived at my destination tired, trembling and prey to anyone who offered to carry it for me. Gallingly, I knew all about the advantages of travelling light; but the pressure of time had turned me into a fool. Before leaving Australia, I had been too busy to pay attention to what I packed and so had crammed absurd, extraneous items into my case: two left thongs, heavy books, winter suits. I had abandoned some items in Athens; some, I had posted home; others, I had dumped. Even so, a millstone remained. I mentally rehearsed the routine ahead: dragging my case onto the bus to Skala Eresou, dragging it off again, and then dragging it to my hotel room. This protracted folly – my clumsy metaphor for an overloaded life – had gone on for long enough. I brushed away my *tiropita* crumbs and fear of driving, and decided to hire a car.

Lesbos is one of the biggest islands in the Aegean. It has a permanent population, a private life, and its citizens produce excellent ouzo and olive oil, away from the insatiable eyes of the tourist. Mytilini itself is crowded, grimy and car-choked; an ugly incongruity on an otherwise lovely island, and one that is typically Greek. I wondered if the noise and chaos was an inevitable part of any Greek city because it represented an unconscious Greek ideal (the clamour, the sense of unforseen possibilities), just as Australians can be relied upon to build towns permeated by a lonely, tree-lined hush.

Once I had left Mytilini, I drove through a rolling landscape of densely planted olive trees. The topography of Lesbos lacks the drama of other islands: the steep peaks have the space to stretch out, to undulate and create more subtle allurements. Skala Eresou was a ninety-kilometre drive away, to the west. The further I drove, the flintier the landscape became, as the dark olive groves slowly gave way to spare, stony hills crowned with thorny-flowered oak trees; boulders occasionally thrust their way through the topsoil. The landscape took on an expansiveness, a mythic quality. I could imagine medieval pilgrims with their cloaks and long staffs walking over the rocky hillocks, under an immense sky.

This sense of a medieval quest was reinforced by the monasteries, which were the most substantial landmarks along the road. The biggest was the Leimonos Monastery, founded in 1523 by the metropolitan of Mithymna, St Ignatius. From a distance, the monastery looked grand and imposing, but on closer inspection there were signs of dereliction everywhere. The main building was three storeys high, with wings of monastic cells enclosing a courtyard, but what was once a thriving centre had now largely been abandoned. Some of the cells, including that of St Ignatius, were being restored, and the rubble and detritus around the site reinforced the sense of decay. I asked a woman at a souvenir stall how many monks still lived in the monastery; five, she said, and two of them were very old.

Leimonos had the third largest collection of manuscripts in the Greek Orthodox world (after Mount Athos and Patmos), but its museum had the dusty, makeshift look of a converted scout hall. The remains of saints were stored in silver boxes in a glass case and labelled with a felt-tip pen. In the courtyard, a group of Greek tourists, mostly middle-aged women, were angrily dismayed to learn that their sex prevented them from entering the monastery's main church. "I've been in there before," one of them shouted, "and nothing happened to the church or to me!" But the monks refused to give way, even as the monastery gave way around them.

Just before I reached Skala Eresou, I saw another monastery perched high on a stony peak. Moni Ipsilou was built from the same material as the mountain it stood upon. The mountain stones, the monastery walls and the clouds above them were all varying shades of grey, and it was difficult to tell where one ended and the other began. As the clouds parted, the building looked as though it was emerging out of the sky. It reminded me of a sorcerer's castle or a dragon's lair; a place that sprang from the earth, but fed the imagination.

><

Professor Ignatius P. Papazoglou arrived promptly at my hotel to take me on a walking tour of Ancient Eresos. The professor had responded to a call from my hotel owner, who had thought of him when I'd asked if he knew anyone who was acquainted with the history of the area. Professor Papazoglou was the ideal guide, he told me. The honorary director of the Teaching Academy of Mytilini, he had been born at Eresos, he had written books about it, he had been instrumental in setting up the small local museum and he had attended the town's only archaeological dig.

The professor's goddaughter worked as a maid at the hotel. She greeted her godfather cheerily, and remarked that she had not once visited any of the town's historic sites, even though they were just outside her door, and wasn't it funny how all the foreigners were so crazy about them? She was interrupted by a man in the lobby, who proclaimed that Eresos was steeped in history, and that the great Sappho herself had taught on Vigla, the very hill before us on the beach.

No, said Professor Papazoglou, that was not true; Sappho never taught at Eresos. He seemed a cheerful man, lacking in self-importance, and was presumably accustomed to the historical indifference of the villagers. But when the man in the lobby began to argue the point, the professor's temper frayed.

"They'd know what they were talking about if they'd read my books," he muttered as we set out for the archaeological museum. On the way, we collected his brother-in-law, Tassos, a furniture salesman from Mytilini, who was washing his car on the street.

"Forget that and come with us," said the professor abruptly, "you might learn something." Tassos, a smiling, ironic fellow, dropped his sponge and obeyed.

The museum was a small building filled with artefacts: inscribed tablets, broken columns, little ceramic vases, measuring cups from an ancient grocer. A grave stele from the classical period was the prize exhibit: a husband's solemn farewell to his seated wife, made in a time before mourners found consolation in dreams of heaven. Next door was the archaeological dig: the early Christian Basilica of St Andrew, occupying the site where it is believed a temple of Apollo once stood.[†]

Professor Papazoglou told me that Ancient Eresos had also boasted temples to Poseidon and Dionysos, as well as an agora and a stadium. The town had been one of the great cities of Lesbos, famed for its wine and as the place where Hermes was sent to gather wheat for the gods. The professor gestured to Vigla and the surrounding fields. The area was sure to be full of archaeological treasures, lying just a metre or so below the surface, but the lack of funds kept them in the ground.

We picked our way along goat tracks and over grassy fields, in brilliant sunshine. The oak trees that were a common feature of the western part of the island shed their thorny flowers on the ground; they grew in the loneliest spots, usually in formation. I had asked a number of people about them, but no-one knew why the trees had been planted. I picked up a dried oak flower, with an acorn in its heart, and listened to the professor. He was a natural teacher: he enjoyed an audience, enjoyed explaining what he knew. His enthusiastic commentary was occasionally interrupted by Tassos, who was concerned about grass burrs in his socks. "Ignat?" he'd say plaintively. "Where are we going? Where are you taking us, Ignat?"

Our last stop was a tumbledown farmhouse, erected in part from marble scrounged from the ruins. A foundation stone from the basilica lay underneath the stair, its engraved cross placed upside down; a broken column supported the verandah; and the backyard tap dripped onto what appeared to be a Doric capital. The professor rapped on one of the wooden window shutters, but there was no-one at home; only a goat bleated a reply.

The morning ended at Mitso's bar, where I often ate my breakfast. Mitso served good coffee and pancakes, and played Nat King Cole and Peggy Lee, music that had been popular in Sydney when he lived there. He was a melancholy soul. Whenever I praised Skala Eresou, he would respond with a sardonic smile: *if only I knew*. And yet, despite his sadness – or perhaps because of it – he had an oddly compelling charm. He told me he often regretted returning to Greece, but the cause of his regret was hard to fathom. In Sydney he had worked in a metal factory, in a food-processing plant and in a restaurant, where he had spent his days scrubbing saucepans. He described all this in dour, self-mocking tones; he knew that he could hardly be said to have left the big time behind.

Mitso now joined the professor and me for coffee. As he sat down he picked up the thorny flower that I had gathered from beneath the oak trees. "How many years has it been since I saw one of these?" he said, cradling it in his hands.

His voice expressed both bitterness and tenderness. When he was a boy, his family had cultivated the oak flowers, which he called *velonyes*. He had picked them, sorted them, stacked them, and had finally fled to Australia to escape them. The acorns were fed to the pigs, while the flowers were sold to be used in the dying and preservation of leather.

"Now they use chemicals and poison the earth," he said with a grimace, "and that is what will end us all."

Mitso gazed at the flower in his hands, but when I asked him if he wanted to keep it he looked at me as though I were mad, and dropped it on the ground. "I've seen enough of them to last me a lifetime," he said.

><

I wanted to return to Mithymna, a village I had visited with a girlfriend one August, thirteen years before. My memory of our week there had brought me back to Lesbos: the grey stone buildings on a hillside with their views of the water; the steep, narrow main street covered in wisteria vines; and, most of all, the night when there were no beds to be had in the village and we had slept in a field of stubble, under a full moon, listening to the sea.

Having overcome my fear of driving, I had decided to keep the car for the duration of my stay. On a whim I took a detour to Ancient Andissa, because I believed the sign that said it was only three kilometres off the main road, and because I was enjoying meandering around the island. I soon found myself driving behind the sand dunes of a long, deserted beach. The site, when I eventually reached it, consisted chiefly of a derelict fort standing on a raised promontory, with a beach on one side and a protected cove on the other. Wild fennel, oregano and a luxuriant fig grew between the rocks, and in the distance I could see farmers burning off nettles in their fields. Although not far from Skala Eresou, I'd left the tourist belt way behind me; I felt like a time traveller, heading back into the island's rural past.

The roads were now unsealed: I had driven off the map. I drew up beside a farmer and his wife sitting stoically on rush-bottomed chairs, one on either side of their farmhouse. They bustled up to the car, eager to give me directions back to the main road. They had been sitting there, alone with their thoughts, just waiting; our brief chat in the fading light was their afternoon's diversion.

I spent that night in the heart of the olive-growing district. I had intended to stay in Mytilini, but had impulsively followed the signs to Agiasos on Mt Olympus, inspired by an acquaintance in Athens who had described Agiasos as "one of the few beautiful villages left in Greece."

The village was really a small town, steeply situated on the mountainside. The road narrowed as I approached the dense cluster of stone houses and shops, leading me to a vine-covered, brightly lit square, where meat hung on hooks outside the butchers' shops and men stood around the newsstands, smoking and gossiping. It was Saturday evening, the shopping hour – *volta* time. The men stared openly as I drove by, giving me the uncomfortable sensation that I had intruded upon them.

The only pension I could find was at the top of the hill. It was unlit; no-one answered the door. As I walked back to the car, an old lady with a scarf around her head greeted me warmly: "And so you have come to us," she said, taking my hand in the dark, "welcome to our village." She told me that the pension was not closed, but merely unattended; the owner lived nearby. She walked with me to his house, smiling sweetly all the while, before bidding me goodnight.

After I had settled into my room I walked back into the town, passing a butcher's shop that displayed cows' heads, pigs' trotters, sides of pork and a huge lump of beef bleeding slowly onto an enamel plate. Agiasos was a constricted, old-fashioned place. The men in the square lacked the old lady's grace and made no effort to disguise their curiosity about me. Trying to ignore their stares, I bought a bag of apples and some pomegranates before entering a small restaurant.

All the other customers were men who had gathered to watch

a soccer match on television. My entrance caused a hiatus in their talk, and when their chatter resumed I felt that I was still under covert surveillance. A man at a nearby table suddenly began talking loudly in German, to the amusement of everyone else. At first I couldn't tell whether he was trying to say something serious to me or was simply making fun of a stranger. I told him in Greek that I was Australian, and that I didn't understand German; but as he was having some success with his performance, he ignored me and continued his German routine, his voice and gestures unnatural, exaggerated. He reminded me of the man in my father's village who had threatened to kill my husband when he'd first seen us in the street; later, we'd learnt that the man, a returned emigrant, was crazy; the trauma of living abroad had left him unbalanced, and with a lifelong grudge against foreigners. The man in Agiasos may well have had a similar story, but in this case his resentment had spread around the room. The waitress smiled at me, trying to make amends, but whenever she withdrew to the kitchen an atmosphere of subdued hostility remained.

That night my sleep was infected with dreams of claustrophobia, impotence and failure. I woke wanting to escape from Agiasos, convinced that the place had infected my dreams. But that impulse was balanced by a desire to leave with a good impression of the village. It was Sunday, so I decided to attend the service at the village church; I walked down to the square as the bells rang out.

The church was full of women; this was their domain, just as the square, the restaurant and the cafes were male territory. Greek churches are usually social places: a low murmur of greetings and chat hums over the congregation, children run up and down the aisles and men cluster around the doorway, finishing their

107

cigarettes. But a heavy, self-conscious piety hung over the women at Agiasos; the atmosphere was as unwelcoming as the mood in the square had been the night before.

Most of the women were sitting on the left side of the church; a few men sauntered in during the latter part of the service, taking the less crowded pews on the right. Their studied casualness made a sharp contrast to the intense, emotional mood that surrounded the women. About halfway through the service, a middle-aged woman stood up and systematically genuflected before all the icons of the iconostasis. Then she walked down towards the entrance, only to turn around and make her way back up the central aisle on her knees. A much younger woman followed suit, bearing a tall candle and trailed by her mother, who was blind. The mother, in turn, clung to the arm of her son, who guided her with an air of smiling unconcern, as though unconnected with his family's fervour.

Later I learned that pilgrims visit the Agiasos church because they believe that its icon of the Virgin has healing powers. To make their way up the aisle on their knees is an act of devotion, or *tami*, a type of spiritual payment performed by those whose prayers have been answered and by those who hope that they will be. Men may also perform a *tami*, but it is traditionally women's business. Knowing nothing of this at the time, however, I took the ritual humiliation I witnessed that morning at face value; it saddened and disturbed me.

It was a relief to step outside into the sunshine, but the square held its own oppressions. I sat down outside a cafe to order a morning coffee, and immediately regretted it: what I really wanted to do, with a rising sense of urgency, was to get up and leave town.

><

The olive is a blessed tree. Hardy and long-lived, with fruit that is nourishing and useful, it is an intrinsic part of Greek cuisine and of Greek domestic life. The oil is used in delicate filo pastry; in bean and lentil soups; in sweet *kourambyedes*. It is used to dress salad, to baste meat, to moisten bread, to soften the skin, to make soap. Olive oil feeds the lanterns in roadside shrines and in grand cathedrals; it polishes the red eggs of Easter and anoints the baby in baptism. In myth, the olive tree was wise Athena's gift to the people of Attica. The olive branch is an ancient symbol of peace, but for Greeks, more particularly, the olive is also a symbol of domestic harmony. Olive oil is sacred, as bread is sacred. Like bread, it represents both poverty and wealth; the most meagre rations include it, and no feast would be complete without it. The olive is a sign of modest attainment, for it is said that the smallest landowner will get by if he can produce enough oil for his table. The olive also stands for the land. The tree has been cultivated for as long as people have lived in Greece; both survive on stony ground. To a patriot, the olive is as bitter and necessary as Greek history: a reminder of hard times; a source of sustenance and continuity, of comfort and inspiration. The trees spring wild from the Greek soil; the roots go deep.

Olives are a winter crop. By mid-October, the residents of Mithymna and the neighbouring seaside town of Petra were beginning to spread their tarpaulins in the olive groves to catch the falling fruit. The sight reminded me immediately of my father's village. The olive groves brought back memories of the farming routines and the domestic entanglements that awaited me there, and nostalgia for the place rushed back with a familiar ache. I also noted – approvingly – the civilising effect the olive tree continues to have in Greece. In these coastal villages on Lesbos tourism is intense and reliable, and yet the olive harvest continues. The olives slow the winter migration to Athens and Mytilini; they provide a balance to the year.

As it was the tail end of the season, hotel prices were low. I found an elegant, self-contained apartment in a block bordering a newly planted olive grove. My room was opposite the beach at Eftalou, just out of Mithymna, with views of the sea and of the Turkish coast. Ever since I left Patmos, I had been skirting Turkey. Although its territory was so close, it was also absurdly remote: ferries travelled across the border, but ticket prices were inflated by steep customs fees; the Turkish-controlled islands of Tenedos and Imroz were nearby, but excluded from Greek maps and ferry routes; Greek ferries did not make the trip up the Dardanelles to Istanbul (although Greek chartered yachts did).

In Mithymna's archaeological museum, the most touching exhibits were only eighty-three years old: framed black-and-white photographs of the Turks leaving Lesbos in November 1912. The deposed occupiers piled into wooden boats crammed with bedrolls and packs; Greek soldiers stood along the water-front in front of a building's burned-out shell. The Turks wore balaclavas and scarves to keep warm. Although they were making just a short trip across the strait to what was notionally their homeland, the journey signalled the beginning of a lifelong exile. Already, each passenger had the hollow, worn look of a refugee.

The museum was in the basement of a neo-classical building that also served as Mithymna's town hall. Upstairs, in a cool, shuttered room, was the office of the mayor, Vathis Dimitrios, a dark-haired, dark-skinned, dark-browed man, handsome and articulate. A native of the town, he had returned to Mithymna after an exile of his own making. For fifteen years he had studied and worked as an electrical engineer in the United States, where he had been employed by General Electric's scientific research centre in North Carolina. His hunger for an intellectual challenge had driven him abroad.

"I couldn't pursue what I wanted to do in Greece. My job in the States was something I would not have left for anything. But," – and here he spread his hands and smiled – "I came to the point where I did leave it."

He left because his daughters were ready to begin high school. He had been alarmed by the example of his sister's daughter, who had been born in the States and married an American. His niece still spoke Greek, but her children did not; he did not want his own grandchildren to share that fate.

Back in Mithymna Mr Dimitrios had built a hotel on the outskirts of town, on land he had inherited from his family; the hotel was his livelihood now. He said he had no regrets about his decision to return: the Greek way of life made more sense to him. In the second half of his life, Mithymna offered him what the States could not: simple conviviality. "To go out regularly with your friends at night – now that is group therapy, something that doesn't exist elsewhere. That is why there are no psychiatrists here. We talk about our problems, our plans, our children. We talk about what troubles us, and what do we see? That our problems are shared by other people, that they are not ours alone; and that knowledge helps us not to worry."

But he admitted that the transition back to life in Greece had not been entirely smooth; bureaucracy had been a constant bugbear, particularly in the early years of setting up his business. The effects of lifelong tenure for public servants and the hazards inherent in any bureaucracy combine hellishly in Greece; only the wealthy and powerful are immune. Smiling thinly, Mr Dimitrios said that in order to build his hotel, "I had to navigate the forty waves, as they say." His chief tormentor had been a clerk in the Greek National Tourist Organisation, who had the job of approving the architectural plans for his hotel. Mr Dimitrios sent the plans, with all the requisite specifications, to Athens and then telephoned to ask how long approval would take. He was told that his plans were number 1000 on the list, and that they were now processing application number 80. They suggested he ring back in a month. And so, "like a good little American," that is what he did. And he rang the month after that, and the month after that, and the month after that. Finally, in the fifth month, Mr Dimitrios set off for Athens to enquire about his plans in person.

"I'm sorry, I still can't help you," the clerk told him. "I am still not up to number 1000." But, as luck would have it, Mr Dimitrios happened to see the application on the public servant's desk: it was number 1015.

"What's this?" he asked.

"I just pulled it out for a quick check," said the clerk.

"Well, pull mine out for a quick check."

"I will in due course."

"Good, I'll wait for you." Mr Dimitrios then pulled up a chair and watched the man work. He stayed there for three days.

"Eventually, he couldn't work with me sitting there. By which I mean that he was accustomed to not working very hard, but with me there he had to put on a show of working. And so, finally, he said to me, 'I'll look at your file.' And do you know how long it took him? Fifteen minutes. He opened it, he read it, he signed it and I left."

Mr Dimitrios told me that his daughters were both studying abroad: the older girl was in the United States, pursuing her aptitude for mathematics, while the younger one was in England studying business administration. He was confident that the younger girl would return, as she would be able to find tourism work in Mithymna; but he feared that his elder daughter would stay away, as he had, and for much the same reasons.

Mithymna was as charming as I remembered, but it had also become a different place. The fishing village had metamorphosed into a wealthy and sophisticated resort; only a skeleton of the village fleet remained and serious fishing was supplemented with moonlight fishing cruises for the visitors. Although the historic old town was protected by Government decree, big hotels proliferated in the surrounding countryside. Mr Dimitrios told me that he believed development in the district had reached a critical point: further construction would make the town too crowded, and whatever charm it still retained would be lost. The transformation of the town was already irreversible; the fields of stubble where I had once spent the night now existed only in memory.

><

I wanted to return to my father's village, but at the same time I was reluctant to leave Mithymna and Lesbos and the sea. In planning this leg of my journey, I had imagined that visiting the islands would be like choosing between so many pearls on a string, and I had deliberately chosen a route that would take me further and further out over the Aegean. I had wanted to be satiated by the sea; to know how it felt to sleep over it, to eat by it, to swim in it, for days and weeks on end. And when the time came to say goodbye to the islands, what I regretted most was not leaving a particular person or place, but letting go of this watery fancy. Despite the wind and the heedless crowds and the crazy ferry routes, I did not want to give up the world of the sea.

I left Mytilini on the *Theophilos*, a big ferry incongruously decorated with large colour photographs of Tasmania; my blue-and-red cabin featured a photo mural of the Hobart casino. The ferry pulled out at dusk, to the accompaniment of a German jazz band playing on the cruise ship moored next to us. Our siren sounded, and the Germans stopped dancing on the deck and lined up to wave: goodbye, goodbye. It was ridiculous, but touching too. People were waving at us from the harbour as well, and some of the passengers began to cry. Caïques bobbed in the stretch of sea beyond the port, black outlines against the setting sun. I strained my eyes to count them, unwilling to lose sight of the men in their little boats who would always have that view, who belonged there, in the fading light of the purple Aegean.

* Between 1897 and 1906, scholars working at Oxyrhyncus found fragments of Sappho's poems among mummy-wrappings made from papyrus, including the mummy-wrapping of a crocodile. Byzantine scholars are believed to have been the last to have had contact with her complete works; one theory has it that their copies were destroyed by fire in 1204 when Constantinople was sacked by marauding Catholics of the Fourth Crusade. Another theory is that the works were destroyed because Christians found Sappho's subject matter morally repugnant.

† A modern church has been built directly behind the basilica. All that remains of the basilica is its pebble mosaic floor; marble scattered around the perimeter probably comes from the temple of Apollo, demolished to make way for the new God. Ironically, the religion that brought the old world to an end now forms the only visible continuity with the past at Skala Eresou. The site where the temple of Athena once stood also remains sacred, and is occupied by a small Orthodox chapel.

PART TWO

BORDERLANDS

What shall I send you, my dear one, there in the Underworld?
If I send you an apple, it will rot, if a quince, it will shrivel;
If I send grapes, they will fall away, if a rose, it will droop.
So let me send my tears, bound in my handkerchief.

from 'The Lament', anonymous folksong

Chapter Six

To the Imperial City

I TOOK THE TRAIN to Istanbul on an impulse. The city may not be in Greece, but it continues to loom large in the Greek psyche. Whenever a Greek conjures up the past, Constantinople – the continuing use of the old name is significant – is there: the golden metropolis that straddles two worlds. Istanbul's population is now greater than the population of Greece, and yet the city – not as it is, but as it was – continues to exert a powerful influence on the Greek imagination.

My family in the Peloponnese, secure on a peninsula that is incontestably Greek, regarded my venture into Turkey and Thrace, the neck of land bordering that country, with some alarm. "Wild and unlawful people live up there," said my uncle Apostoli, pointing vaguely towards the Corinthian Gulf and the hazy mountains of Roumeli in the distance. "Double your eyes – *ta matya sou tesera* – and don't go out at night."

"Don't eat the sausage in Thrace," warned Dimitri, the taxi driver and distant cousin who often drove me up and down the mountain road that ran between my father's village and the seaside town of Egira. He said he knew of people who had been poisoned by unsavoury Thracian meats, hinting darkly that such events were not always accidental. And as for Turkey: if I were foolhardy enough to go there, the only safe course, he believed, was to drink only bottled water and not to eat at all.

For centuries, in the Byzantine and then in the Ottoman world, Istanbul was known simply as 'the City', as though the world knew no other. Its era of greatness began in 330 AD, when the Roman emperor Constantine moved his court to what until then had been the Greek settlement of Byzantium. Constantine, the first Roman emperor to embrace Christianity, recast the city as the successor to Rome. Constantinople's citizens called themselves *romaioi* – Romans – even after Greek replaced Latin as the official language of the court; it is a tradition that persists among the Greeks to this day. For more than 1100 years, Constantinople was the religious, political and cultural capital of an empire. Its people believed that their city was uniquely blessed by God and that it flourished under His protection. They covered their church domes and city gates with gold so that Constantinople would resemble the heavenly Jerusalem; their emperor was known as *isapostle* – the equal of an Apostle – and was held to be Christ's representative on earth in worldly affairs. Even when defeat came to the city on a Tuesday in May 1453, sections of the Church interpreted the Ottoman occupation as a kind of perverse victory for Orthodox Christianity. It was argued that the religiously tolerant Turks formed part of a grand design to protect Orthodoxy until such time as the Greek Church could be restored to its rightful greatness, Constantinople having still not recovered from the Latin barbarities of the Fourth Crusade. The belief echoed an esoteric Byzantine apocalyptic tradition which prophesied that Alexander would rise again to unite the Greeks before the end of time.

And here was a tragic irony, for the Greeks did rise to conquer again, but in a manner unforeseen by the Church that had made it possible. For the preceding millennium, Byzantine monks had preserved classical manuscripts unknown to a Europe living through the Dark Ages. In the empire's dying days, influential scholars moved west to disseminate these works, works that played a part in the Renaissance rediscovery of classical antiquity that had already begun without them. But the ancient scripts would bear no more fruit in Constantinople.

><

My cousin Bill was to accompany me on part of this northern journey. A writer and translator, he had spent the summer in the village while completing his second novel. He had only a scant interest in politics – a rare quality in a Greek – and so as a companion and occasional interpreter could be relied upon to remain relatively objective and detached. I was looking forward to spending some time with Bill again as we had not seen each other for eight years. He had recently recovered from a serious illness and he carried the vulnerable look of a person who is newly discovering their own fitness. He had grown thinner and looked warier, more guarded than I remembered. Although he said he was keen to come with me, his voice could not disguise its apparently habitual trace of weary resignation.

We arrived in Istanbul after a twenty-five-hour overland trip by train and bus. It had not been possible to take a train all the way because Turkish rail services had been suspended, a consequence of a public-service strike that was in its seventh month. An overnight Greek train took us from Athens to Alexandroupolis, a port town near the border, where we connected with a privately run Turkish bus.

The journey began promisingly enough. In the autumn sunshine, the train wound its way over the undulations of central Greece as Bill and I debated whether we were in the most beautiful country in the world. Bill had recently spent six weeks in Nepal and said the Himalayan kingdom was as "lovely as fairyland." But Greece made her case silently as the train travelled through tunnels and over the rocky passes north of Lamia. The Greek mountains are not as inspirational as the Himalayas, but they are nearly always blessed with views of the sea. By the end of the day we had agreed that the Greek combination was hard to beat.

For our journey, Bill had purchased a mobile phone "in case people need to talk to me" – a move that had provoked uncharitable eyebrow-raising from our family. "What does he expect, a movie offer?" Now, as we travelled through the outskirts of Thessaloniki, the phone rang. It was a film director, asking Bill to submit a script proposal for a Greek road movie. The director said he wanted gritty realism; he would give Bill artistic freedom, but could he possibly include a scene involving top models in a hotel? The call provided a distraction from the train's sad lack of a restaurant car, a circumstance that had reduced us to an evening meal of bottled water and cream crackers. In his movie, Bill assured me, the characters would fare better than this.

We spent the night in a creaky sleeping car and pulled into Alexandroupolis at dawn. The town is only forty kilometres from the border and has a raw, lonely, neglected look. We sat out the cold hours of the sunrise at a *kafeneion*, drinking double Turkish coffees with evaporated milk and eating *bougatses* from a shop that was mercifully open on a Sunday morning. (*Bougatses*, a northern Greek speciality, are filo-pastry pies filled with custard, served warm and sprinkled with cinnamon. Delicious.)

I asked the man in the *bougatsa* shop if he had been to Istanbul; after all, Alexandroupolis was closer to the great city than it was to Athens.

"No, never," replied the wiry, grey-haired fellow, deftly slicing the pie into bite-sized pieces with a metal spatula.

"Why not?"

"I have never had the time," and he flung out his hand to indicate his shop: his livelihood, his prison. I had briefly forgotten how lucky we were to have escaped, even if for a short time, the tyranny of a daily routine.

After two hours the Turkish bus turned up to take us to the border, a flat and swampy stretch of land where we waited for two hours more. The place looked anonymous and hopeless; a purgatory of sorts. A mood of bureaucratic cussedness predominated as customs officials from both sides played out a pantomime of mutual distrust by holding on to our passports for as long as possible.

In the queue on the Turkish side, a dapper Greek-speaking man from our bus stood just ahead of me. He held a Turkish passport and I discovered that he was an Orthodox priest based in Istanbul. A black-clad Greek woman standing near us took it upon herself to tell me, in a conspiratorial whisper, that in Turkey members of the Orthodox clergy were legally obliged to wear civilian dress in public. "Call him Father," she urged. The Father said he was one of about forty Orthodox priests still performing the liturgy in Istanbul and that only a few thousand Greeks now lived in the city. ("They slaughtered all the rest in '55," whispered the woman.) I wanted to continue the conversation, but the priest politely declined.

Later, during a rest stop, Bill also approached him, without success. The cleric looked around cautiously and bowed his head. "We are the only Christians here," he said softly.

><

To understand the circumstances of the Greeks who remain in Istanbul, a further historical explanation is needed. Following the Balkan wars of 1912 – a brief struggle against the last vestiges of the Ottoman empire – Greece won a military and diplomatic coup. Eleftherios Venizelos, the Greek prime minister at the time, negotiated what was widely regarded as a brilliant settlement, extending the country's borders into what is now southern Epiros and Macedonia, as well as taking in the islands of the northern Aegean; the deal almost doubled Greek territory. With one brief campaign, Greece had gone some way towards achieving what was known as the Great Idea: the post-Independence dream of restoring Greece to its pre-Ottoman outline, including the coast of Asia Minor and the city of Constantinople itself. The Great Idea tapped into a Greek sense of historical destiny that had its roots in Byzantium.

This dream of a greater Greece has cast a long shadow. After its victory in the Balkan wars, the Greek army went on to play a significant though relatively minor role in the First World War, leading Venizelos to believe that the Greek effort had earned his country firm allies in Europe. Whether Venizelos was deliberately misled by the Allies' promises of land in Asia Minor (Anatolia), or whether he made a tragic miscalculation, is still debated. In 1921 – when Venizelos was no longer prime minister – Greece attempted to 'liberate' Asia Minor; by June the Greek army had advanced as far as the River Sakarya on the road to Ankara. Here the Turkish general Kemal Ataturk counter-attacked and successfully held back the invading Greeks.

Greece's foothold in Asia Minor was the coastal city of Smyrna (known today as Izmir), which it had occupied in May 1919 in the name of the Allies. The rich mercantile port was dubbed the city of infidels by the Turks, as it was mostly populated by non-Islamic peoples: Greeks, Armenians and Jews. In September 1922, the Turks retook the city. Houses and shops were sacked and looted, and the wooden city burned, many of the Greek inhabitants running into the sea to escape the flames. Some thirty thousand Christians perished. Within ten days, 2500 years of a continuous Greek presence on the shores of the eastern Aegean had ended.

In Greece, these events are still referred to as the Asia Minor Catastrophe. Its diplomatic resolution was the Treaty of Lausanne, signed by Greece and Turkey in July 1923, which ceded western Thrace to Greece. The treaty also involved a massive compulsory population exchange between the two countries, in which Muslims living in Greece were sent to Turkey and Orthodox Christians in Turkey were sent to Greece; in a secular age, religion remained the arbitrary designator of national identity. Orthodox citizens who spoke no Greek were forced to leave their Turkish birthplace, just as Greek-speaking

Muslims, some of whom had converted from Orthodoxy for reasons of political expediency years before, were obliged to move to Turkey. Greece had to absorb more than one million refugees, of whom a disproportionate number were widows and orphans; 380,000 Muslims crossed the border into Turkey.

Exceptions were made for the Muslim population of Thrace and the Orthodox population of Istanbul, who were allowed to stay put.* But in the years since the treaty, the two communities have been rocked by the distrust that has characterised the relationship between the nations. To varying degrees, each has been made to pay. The size of the Muslim population in Greek Thrace has held steady, however, while the Greek Orthodox presence in Istanbul has fallen dramatically. Most people I spoke to estimated that fewer than 5000 Greeks remained in the city. I wanted to get a sense of who these people were and why they had stayed.

><

Kemal strode into our hotel foyer dressed in an elegant chocolate-brown overcoat. Tall, dark and slender, he cut a fine figure. It was Kemal's fervent belief that Turks and Greeks, far from being natural enemies, were brothers tragically separated by religion, history and politics. "No other two peoples on earth have so much in common," he told us, "we are the same."

He delivered this speech at our first meeting, perched on the edge of an armchair, his long legs doubled up uncomfortably behind a coffee table. He spoke persuasively and at length, pausing only to refuse a cup of the hotel tea (a wise move). His conversation was marked by a disarming sincerity, expressed by a look of quivering intensity around the eyes.

Bill had contacted Kemal on the advice of a mutual friend, who had described him as an excellent fellow, a lawyer with an enthusiasm for Greeks. It was Sunday evening, but Kemal – who knew nothing of us and who had been given no notice of our arrival – had met us within thirty minutes of receiving Bill's call. He shook our hands warmly and welcomed us to Istanbul; he was at our service.

Kemal spoke English and Greek, but said – without irony – that he preferred Greek because English was the language of capitalist imperialists. His Greek was halting but impeccable, the result of years of self-tuition; for the first five years he had ploughed on without the benefit of conversation practice because he had known no Greeks. Greek politics and history had been his sole inspiration.

What did the Greeks and Turks have in common? So much, so much – he intertwined his fingers to demonstrate what he meant. They shared hundreds of years of history. The two peoples looked alike; much of their traditional music and dance was the same; the cuisines were similar; the two languages had many words in common; and the people's customs, while not identical, were alike in spirit – and here he cited the law of hospitality as his example.

He paused and leaned forward, earnestly pressing his finger-tips together. Did we agree with him? If we did not, we would by the time we left Istanbul. In the meantime, it seemed he was prepared to sit in the foyer, without tea or sustenance of any kind, answering our questions for as long as we wished. But it was getting late and we had not eaten a proper meal since our breakfast *bougatses*. When asked if he could recommend a restaurant, Kemal leapt to his feet, exclaiming yes, yes, yes, he

127

knew just the place. Outside it was raining, but no matter, he would drive us there immediately.

Our hotel was in Sultanahmet, the historical and tourist precinct near Hagia Sophia, but Kemal's instinct was to head for the more aristocratic district near the Pera Palace Hotel, on the other side of the Golden Horn. In the car he played a compilation tape of *rembetika* music, the so-called Greek blues of the 1920s, another of his enthusiasms. He hummed along to an odd little song about garlic sauce and fried fish as he drove us through Istanbul's dark, near-deserted streets. I strained out of the rain-streaked windows, hoping to catch a glimpse of the city's floodlit domes and minarets. We had arrived at twilight, and had as yet barely seen Istanbul; our most memorable impression so far had been the concrete skeletons of new suburbs that stretched drably to the horizon on the outer edges of town. When I mentioned them to Kemal he abruptly broke off his song. Istanbul's best days were over, he said. Whatever charm remained was being choked by the flood of rural immigrants – many tens of thousands each year – which the Government had so far been powerless to check.

Kemal spoke about his country with all the bitter cynicism of a disillusioned patriot (he wore a discreet silver pin of Ataturk's profile on the lapel of his jacket). Tansu Çiller's Government, which was then in power, disgusted him, and he also abhorred the growing popularity of the Islamic party. "Turkey is on a train, in a dark tunnel, and there is no light at the end of it," he remarked, and then laughed immoderately at his analogy, as though it were a joke.

The restaurant was a modest, simply furnished place in a lane off a main street. Kemal ordered for us all, and we spent the next two hours sampling a selection of carefully prepared dishes while drinking a 1985 Semillon grown near the Sea of Marmara. "Turks say that we do not have democracy, but we do have good wine," quipped Kemal as he filled our glasses.

Turkish cuisine is more delicate, more complex and more varied than Greek fare, whose combination of seasonal produce and strong, simple flavours can appear somewhat artless. The Turks use a similar range of ingredients but they are subtler, more refined cooks. Our meal began in the traditional way with bread, dips, vegetable dishes and salads; we were hungry and ate greedily. A buttery mushroom and cheese *burek* or pie came next. Hunger was now satisfied, but the courses kept coming: croquettes, poultry, shaslik, potatoes, braised meat, pilaf . . . Kemal had ordered an overabundance of riches.

Sometime between the second and third courses, a small band of Turkish classical musicians entered the room and began to play. Bill knew the Greek words to many of the songs but I could not recognise any. To my untrained ear the lilting, mellifluous tunes flowed into each other; the drama and emphasis of Greek music were missing. I remarked that the violinist looked sad, and Bill and Kemal, who shared an interest in music, replied together: "It's because the drummer is too loud." Soon all the diners had been seduced and were softly singing along. Two pretty young women at the opposite table closed their eyes and joined in dreamily; Bill sang in Greek and Kemal in Turkish.

I hesitated over a plate of apple, cinnamon and purple pomegranate seeds. We were now onto our third bottle of wine. In my intoxicated state, the songs, the wine and the food all mingled, flowing together in a languid stream of flavours and melodies. The music washed over me. I lacked the will to resist it.

><

The next morning our inevitable hangovers induced a shared mind-fog. Outside the rain continued to fall, and I had the uncomfortable sensation that my brain too was shrouded in a wet cloud. Bill had the added discomfort of a dull ache in his liver. Because of his recent illness he was not supposed to drink more than one glass of wine a day. "But last night," he explained unnecessarily, "it was impossible to drink only one glass."

Over breakfast, we decided to visit the office of the Ecumenical Patriarch, the head of the Eastern Orthodox Churches, in order to make an appointment with the Patriarch or his nominated spokesman. I thought it unlikely that anyone would agree to see us immediately, and we could return when our heads were clearer.

The Greek Patriarch performs a dual role. On the one hand he is a Turkish citizen and the religious leader of the country's diminished Orthodox population; as such he is nominated by the Church and appointed by the Turkish Government as an official in the Directorate of Religious Affairs. But he is also the leader of the Orthodox Church as a whole. He therefore oversees a contradiction, for as the population of the Istanbul diocese shrinks, so the number of Orthodox faithful around the world grows, particularly in the former Eastern bloc.

We headed for the Fener district, the home of the patriarchate since about 1600. This precinct is still known by the Greeks as Phanari – the lighthouse or lantern – as it was a famous centre of Greek wealth and influence during the Ottoman empire. Now, however, its streets were little more than slums. The ornate, multi-storeyed houses, once the homes of influential diplomats, politicians and intellectuals, were derelict. Families camped within their shells, the occasional flue from a wood-fire stove poking out of a high window; curious children stared down at us from behind shabby curtains. The stone walls of the patriarchate stood near the water's edge; behind the walls was a toehold of privilege, with little relevance to the world immediately surrounding it.

Two portly guards stood gossiping in Greek near the entrance. The Patriarch was unavailable, they said; he was preparing to leave for Romania, but they believed that his second in command, the impressively titled Megas Protosynklitos, would be able to see us. Without ceremony, or a request for identification and credentials, the guards waved us in. A metal detector in the courtyard beeped as we walked through; the guards told us to ignore it and keep walking.

Desperately trying to ignore our hangovers, we waited in an antechamber hung with pictures, including a view of the interior of Hagia Sophia. After a few minutes, we were ushered into a room furnished with antiques and red velvet curtains. The obligatory portrait of Ataturk hung on one wall, while a photograph of the Patriarch was displayed on another. Behind the desk was a moody, gilt-framed landscape of storm clouds, a river and a lighthouse; it was the only object in the room that spoke of Orthodoxy's position in Turkey, and even then through a metaphor that may have only resided in my imagination.

The Megas Protosynklitos was smoking a cigarette and had not yet finished his morning coffee; I immediately noticed his tiny, carefully manicured hands. Dressed in the black robes of the Church, he was short and balding, and had the remote, careful air of a politician. Occasionally the mobile phone on his desk would ring; he was evidently arranging a flight to Paris, and also attending to some business in Tel Aviv.

The Megas Protosynklitos had been born in Istanbul. He was unwilling to talk about the decline of the Greek population in the city, saying he had been only a child during the infamous riots of September '55, and intimating that his memories of the event were therefore not worth mentioning. The riots occurred during tense negotiations over Cyprus; Greek businesses and homes were looted, and livelihoods destroyed. Afterwards, the Greeks affected had the legal right to sue for compensation, but many chose simply to leave the country. ("Once a porcelain cup is broken, it is never the same again," had been Kemal's summing up of the events.)

"It is natural for Greeks to live here," was the Megas Protosynklitos's bland observation; he estimated that between four and a half and five thousand Greeks were left in the city. The statistic, however, was irrelevant to the presence of the patriarchate: its location in Istanbul was an immovable tradition of Orthodoxy. A flicker of impatience crossed his face as he pointed out that the Orthodox Church also had a presence in Jerusalem, a city with a negligible Greek population to service. The presence of the Church in Istanbul was tied to history, not to demographics.

A hairline crack appeared in the cleric's impassive facade when I asked him about the rise of Islamic fundamentalism in Turkey. The muscles of his face stiffened and he stared at me for a short time, without speaking at all. No, he replied eventually, he had no public comment to make on that issue. He did not believe that the movement would affect the patriarchate.

There was only one issue of concern to the Church that the Megas Protosynklitos was willing for me to pursue. It regarded the fate of a theological school that had once been the world's oldest; he had attended it himself before the Turkish Government closed it down in 1971, when he had been forced to finish his studies in Thessaloniki and Paris. He recommended that I pay the school a visit and speak to its head, Bishop Germanos, who lived outside Istanbul on the island of Chalki.

><

We made our way to the ferry in the drizzling rain. Bill was slightly awed to have met the Megas Protosynklitos: "Do you have any idea how important he is?" he asked me more than once as we walked. My temerity in approaching such a personage while hung over had unsettled him.

Walking through Istanbul's streets was mesmerising; the city offered a greater wealth of sensations than I could take in at once. The place was bigger, more alluring and more elusive than I was prepared for. It was an entire world; you could dive into its cobbled lanes and lose yourself there. We passed a *burek* shop, the filled rolls of filo pastry coiled like snakes in the window; a wooden van piled high with split pomegranates; a boat lurching on the Bosphorus, a rolling home for a giant barbecue of sizzling fish; an old man patiently turning the chestnuts on his brazier near a crumbling stone building with a fig tree growing out of its roof . . .

At the quay, we were unable to work out which ferry to catch to Chalki. A young man watched us dither around the various terminals before taking charge of the situation by guiding us onto the nearest departing vessel. "It's OK, it's OK!" he shouted when Bill tried to ask him if this was the boat for Chalki. We didn't believe him, but acquiesced as a ferry ride was a good opportunity to see the city from a seated vantage point.

We hadn't been prepared for Istanbul's chilly autumn weather. Aboard the ferry we huddled inside, crouched near a heater, our faces pressed to the window as the European coast receded: the domes and minarets of Hagia Sophia and its elegant Ottoman echo, the Blue Mosque; the Topkapi Palace; the Grand Bazaar; and the ornate pile of nineteenth-century commercial buildings crowded along the waterfront. The further away we moved, the more the city beckoned, its size and its intricacy benefiting from the widest possible view.

Of course the ferry was not heading for Chalki at all; after fifteen minutes it arrived at the Asian coast, where everyone disembarked except us. On the journey back to Europe we drank sweet tea from glass cups. Opposite us, a Turkish woman in a blue scarf sipped hot milk sprinkled with nutmeg. Next to her sat her husband, his arm around her, and a teenage girl, whom I guessed was their daughter. The girl's face was streaked with tears and the woman spoke to her softly and intently throughout the trip. As sometimes happens, I felt an instinctive sympathy for them all, one that I was unable to express and could not show. I looked away and out the window, and as I did so I noticed the father stealing a surreptitious glance at me: I was not the only one to be confronted by an impenetrable world.

><

We were to meet Kemal for dinner again that night. I told Bill that as Kemal had insisted on paying for our first banquet together, I was determined that our second meal would be my treat. Bill understood my desire to return Kemal's hospitality, but he was also slightly amused at my anxiety to 'pay Kemal back'. He pointed out that no-one had compelled Kemal to spend his money, and that if I insisted on returning the favour, I ran the risk of insulting him; the idea ran counter to the spirit of unstinted hospitality in which Kemal was indulging.

"I like Kemal," Bill concluded, "and I had a good time last night, but I hate all this hospitality stuff, it usually turns out to be bullshit." I had some sympathy for Bill's views. After only one dinner we had become so tangled up in a game of face and good manners that we were embarking on a second big night before we had fully recovered from the first.

When Kemal arrived, wearing a long navy overcoat and his standard lapel pin of Ataturk, I tried a partial save. "I don't know about you, but I would like just a light meal tonight," I told him.

"Yes, yes, of course," said Kemal, but he was smiling in such a way that I knew my request would be ignored. His sense of honour would not allow him to take us out for a mere snack.

Sure enough, the second restaurant was bigger and more elegant than the first, and the patrons were dressed in smarter clothes. It looked like a place that took food seriously: I decided it would be a waste not to enjoy it.

Our first night had been spent talking about food, music and politics, so this time I asked Kemal about himself. He told us that he was thirty, and lived with his mother, who was a judge.

"It's unusual for women to reach such a position in Australia," I said.

"Here it is not so unusual," came the short reply.

Kemal had grown up in a country district near the Black Sea. From childhood, he had felt distanced from his neighbours, from the ordinary folk of his own country. "They had arguments for no reason, they were empty-headed, you could not speak logically to them."

I guessed that this might be the reason why Kemal had developed an interest in Greek people and their culture – because he imagined that they would be different. He himself was at a loss to explain his empathy. "Can you say why you like one piece of music and not another? It is in the person, it is individual taste." Because of his predilection, his Greek friends had made him an honorary Greek and called him Kosta Kalligraphos: Kosta the Well-written. He had once gone out with a Greek girl from Thessaloniki; now he was seeing a Bulgarian girl. His friendships with people of the Orthodox faith had led others to accuse him of being a crypto-Christian, but actually Kemal was an atheist. Atheism was not, he conceded, commonly found among Turks; even his mother, who was not a practising Muslim, believed in a higher power.

I wondered if the relative secularity and scepticism of Greek society was part of its appeal for Kemal. Therein, perhaps, lay the difference between us, as I tried to explain. Coming from a culture which sets great store by order and reason, and where traditional values have declined, I am drawn to the Greeks' tendency to believe in invisible forces, their willingness to give themselves over to emotional and irrational impulses (a trait that is often tempered, paradoxically, by a strongly pragmatic streak). I thought the contrast was neat, with Greece representing an ideal for Kemal that was almost the exact opposite of its attraction for me.

But my argument was soon lost as a river of wine, food and music flooded over us again. Flowing with it was no hardship, although I wished (again) that I'd had the willpower to end my meal with the *burek*. This time Bill and Kemal found fault with the musician playing the *canoni* – a type of stringed instrument – whom they described as selfish and insensitive. But his inadequacies did not prevent the restaurant's patrons – and eventually Bill and Kemal – from swaying and singing along with the band.

When at last it was time to leave, I distracted Kemal with a small subterfuge and managed to pay for the meal. Happily, he conceded my little victory with good grace.

><

The reason Bill and I had been unable to discover which ferry to take to Chalki was simple: Chalki is the island's Greek name, and therefore no longer in general use. Its Turkish name is Heybeliada. One of the so-called Princes' Islands in the Sea of Marmara, it was once a popular holiday destination for Istanbul's wealthy Greeks, Armenians and Jews.

Bishop Germanos was waiting for us. He had given Bill precise directions on the telephone, including the ferry departure times and how much to pay for the horse and carriage that he suggested we hire from the pier. We were expected at 10 am and invited to stay for lunch.

Grey days had dogged us since our arrival in Istanbul. Once we had crossed the border, we had seemingly entered another season. Although the quay was crowded with morning commuters our ferry was almost empty, for who bothers to travel to a summer resort in the off season? Sky and sea swelled with slate-coloured billows as we sat huddled in our coats, looking out at the ever-expanding line of suburbs that stretched along the shore for the length of our eighty-minute journey.

Just as the bishop had said, a horse attached to an incongruously frivolous carriage stood at the end of the Heybeliada pier; we gave our instructions to the driver, who spoke a little Greek. Peering out through the carriage's leather fringes, I saw tree-lined streets and ornate nineteenth-century timber houses.

While still aboard the ferry, we had admired the hilltop seminary, Moni Agias Triados. Now we drew up to the stately three-storey building surrounded by lawns, gardens and greenhouses; there was a chapel and also a small pine forest in the grounds.

An old man in gardening clothes opened the gate.

"This is a beautiful place," I said.

"It's lonely," he replied.

He led us into the empty foyer, up a grand marble staircase and down a long corridor. Bishop Germanos sat by a radiator in his little office. A frail, white-haired man, he greeted us warmly and offered us dried apricots that a friend had sent from the United States. He appeared to be the type of man whose gentle, unassuming manners would have endeared him to any congregation, but he had been ordered to keep watch over an elaborately maintained symbol instead.

The bishop drew sustenance from the Christian ideal. Statements that would have sounded empty or platitudinous from another man had the ring of truth when he made them: "We must love each other," he told us mildly. "We must work for peace. We are all God's children, all brothers in the eyes of God."

He patiently told us the story of the school. The original monastery had been established in the ninth century and had included a library; whatever remained of that medieval collection was now with the patriarchate, but the bishop feared that earthquakes, invasions and the passing of time had all taken their toll. A modern theological school, double-storeyed and made from wood, had been built in 1844, only to be destroyed by an earthquake fifty years later. Then a Greek banker resident in Istanbul had stepped in and donated the money for the school to be rebuilt in its present, grander form.

The seminary had been a combination high school and theological college. It reached its height in the 1950s and '60s, when it had housed 135 students from Greece, Turkey, Cyprus, Egypt, Ethiopia and many other countries; the bishop had studied there himself in 1953 and 1954. He recalled some of the luminaries from his year and how the African students had been popular with the laity because they did not clutter up their sermons with obscure theological arguments.

Classes came to an end in 1971 when the Turkish Government ordered the closure of all private universities run by ethnic minorities. Forty-five high school students stayed on until their graduation; after they left, the teaching staff remained a year longer, but eventually dispersed. The head of the school kept his post until his death in 1991; Mitropolitis Stavroupoleos Maximos had given forty years to Agias Triados. Whenever he had been asked when the school would reopen, he had simply answered: "Tomorrow."

Bishop Germanos was asked to replace him. He had the company of one other cleric, a nominal Turkish director, whom he called *efendi* or master, a librarian and fifteen support staff whose job it was to clean, cook and keep the garden and classrooms in a state of poignant readiness.

The bishop walked us through the echoing rooms: the graduation hall with its wall of portraits and its trompe l'oeil ceiling; the classrooms with black desks in rows like so many untuned pianos; the hall with its cracked tile where generations of boys had split the wood for the classroom combustion heaters. All the rooms were clean and aired; in a dormitory bathroom, new cakes of soap lay on the basins and a row of fresh towels hung from hooks.

Outside a gardener stood in the rain, planting seedlings that only a handful of people would see. Bill exclaimed once again at the loveliness of the setting. "Yes, thanks be to God," said the bishop. "Christ had nowhere to lay his head, but look what the Lord has provided for us." He quietly added that the affairs of Church and state should be kept separate: " 'Render unto Caesar what belongs to Caesar and unto God what belongs to God,' said the Lord." During our morning together it was the only comment the bishop allowed himself to make on the circumstances in which he lived.

Our last stop was the library, where George, one of the few Greeks left on Heybeliada, had recently been employed to transfer the catalogue onto a computer. He showed us room after room of immaculately preserved books: philosophy, theology, history – 50,000 volumes in all. In the periodicals room, recent theological journals and newsletters from around the world were neatly arranged and still tied with string. Leather-bound books lay on a table. We opened one at random: a collection of engravings showing the Palace of Versailles.

"Who comes here?" I asked, although I already knew the answer.

"No-one," said George.

"Which is the oldest book?"

"A typical journalist's question," he replied, before admitting that because he had only worked there a month, he did not know. Also, he was not a librarian. He could only guess at the value of the treasures around him.

><><

That evening Kemal had arranged for us to meet some of his Greek friends: Stavros, a musician who played at the restaurant where we were to dine, and Dimitri, who worked in the shipping industry.

The suburban, seaside restaurant was barnlike and decorated in an impersonal modern style. It doubled as a reception hall, but on this rainy Tuesday evening it was mostly empty. The only other customers were Turks: a table of four middle-aged women on a big night out and an extended family celebrating the birthday of a six-year-old boy. Way back near the kitchen entrance, two men sat drinking beer.

Stavros was in his mid-twenties and had a fresh-faced, like-able boyishness that added to his charm as a performer. He sang well in Greek but spoke the language with an awkwardness that recalled the imprecise kitchen-table Greek of the immigrant child. Whenever Kemal corrected his grammar, which was often, Stavros smiled indulgently. Kemal's intensity was a familiar source of amusement.

Stavros had never been to Greece and said he had no desire to go there. "Why would I want to? I know of some Greeks who went to live in Faliro [a suburb near Piraeus where many Istanbul Greeks have settled] and things didn't go so well with them."

He and his family led a quiet life in Istanbul. His father, who was now dead, had sold ironware – saucepans and such – a modest business that had not been affected by the riots of '55. Stavros's wife was Turkish and so was his boss; his brother and sister had converted to Islam in order to marry Turks.

Stavros was polite enough, but Greece and Turkey was obvi-ously an old story for him and one he preferred to avoid. Greeks irritated him. They were stuck in the past, stuck in a sad replay from long ago. They had too narrow a take on his world to understand it and he was in no mood to be judged by strangers. Earlier in the day on Heybeliada, George had responded in a similar fashion; he too had weighed all my words with distrust and had kept his distance from me.

Stavros was most at ease when we talked about music, because it expressed a truth about who he was and how he lived. About half of the songs he performed were Greek. He spent his days trying to master the bouzouki because his boss had promised him a pay rise if he played it at the restaurant. Greek music was good for business: it was popular, and set the place apart. Sometimes Turks from Greek Thrace came in; they said his songs reminded them of home. In Stavros's experience, Turks had friendly feelings towards Greeks, feelings that were not reciprocated. His gig was his proof: how many musicians performed Turkish music in Athens? Bill admitted that he knew of none.

Kemal, who had been uncharacteristically silent for most of our conversation, nodded in agreement. Turkey, he said, was a developing country with no interest in pursuing hostilities with Greece. "The simple people don't want war . . . They don't understand the Greeks' feelings of animosity towards them."

Stavros opened his set with a lively *tsifteteli*, a flirtatious and feminine dance in which the arms are held over the head and twirled; shoulders shake, hips swivel. At once, the four women from the next table rose and danced joyously; soon they were joined by a young woman from the birthday group.

The women were in a celebratory mood: they danced for the fun of it and for themselves. The best dancer was short, with long, dark hair, almond eyes and broad hips; Bill dubbed her "the lady with no neck." She swayed towards our table smiling genially, her shoulders shimmying and arms outstretched, inviting us to join her. I couldn't resist. It was the first *tsifteteli* I had danced in several years.

When I returned to the table, I saw that Kemal had ordered a half-bottle of *raki* – a clear, potent spirit. "Together we will finish the bottle," he said to Bill.

Bill shook his head: no, that was impossible. Kemal downed a shot and stood up. Stavros was now playing a *hasaposerviko*. Kemal turned to Bill, and with a gesture invited him onto the dance floor. Again Bill shook his head: he never danced. The women had sat down, so Kemal was the only dancer.

The fast-paced *hasaposerviko* is generally danced by a line of dancers. Undeterred, Kemal hooked his left hand behind his neck and flung out his right hand, as though clasping the shoulder of an invisible partner. He looked well, with his long legs, his proud stance and his elegant clothes. And he could really dance. "The man is a true Greek," said Bill admiringly.

As Kemal returned to the table, a man carrying a mobile phone arrived. They embraced and Kemal introduced "Dimitri – my best friend." Dimitri helped himself to the *raki* and then dived onto the dance floor, his arms held out in front of him, jack-knifing jerkily like a small fish. He danced impulsively, with a manic, comic charm. The ladies were back doing the *tsifteteli*, and Dimitri swam around them, making them laugh.

Even though the restaurant was almost empty it was now bursting with *kefi*. This Greek and Turkish word has no direct equivalent in English. ("The English have no word for it because they have no *kefi*," murmured Kemal.) A person with *kefi* is in a mood of lively good cheer; but, more than that, *kefi* can also be a measure of one's capacity for joy and self-forgetfulness. Without *kefi*, dancing is merely a mechanical exercise. It is possible to be filled with *kefi* but to lack a talent for dance – Dimitri was proof of that – but in the best dancers, *kefi* and skill combine; their performance expresses an unselfconscious love of life.

Dimitri spoke better Greek than Stavros, who rejoined us when he finished his set, but he was even more reluctant to talk to me about his life in Istanbul. He made calls on his mobile phone, talked to Stavros at length about how much it would cost to hire the restaurant for a function, and drank more *raki*. In an attempt to engage his interest, I asked him what he thought of the latest developments in Greek Thrace. The Greek media had recently been full of claims and counter-claims about a leaked report that purportedly told of a 'secret' NATO plan to make Greek Thrace an autonomous region. Despite NATO's denial that any such scheme existed, the story ran for days, fleshed out with live crosses to anxious reporters at NATO headquarters and diagrams showing how an autonomous region would aid Turkish plans for an oil pipeline that stretched all the way to the Aegean. Stavros, Dimitri and Kemal all looked at me in astonishment: they had heard nothing about any of this. An awkward silence ensued.

It was eventually broken by Kemal, who asked me whether he had succeeded in his mission: was I convinced that Greeks and Turks were the same? He gestured around him, indicating that our evening in the restaurant should be all the proof I needed. He was edgy: the question was not asked lightly. I knew that if I agreed I would put an easy seal on our friendship and gain the trust of Stavros and Dimitri as well. But instead a complicated jostle of thoughts rose up in my mind: how preconceived ideas – the filter of background or race – only ever tell a partial truth; how it is possible to connect with people without having to agree on a particular this or that; how the strongest ties are invisible and sometimes subversive, flowing under the certainties of politics and history.

And so I hesitated. Looking up, I saw that by doing so I had already lost Kemal. I replied simply that I didn't know if Greeks and Turks were the same. Similarities existed, certainly, but I hadn't met enough people or spent enough time in Turkey to say any more.

Nobody responded. Stavros rose to play his last set, and at Dimitri's request launched into a *zeimbekiko*, a dance often performed by a sole male dancer. Kemal took off his jacket and wedged the bottle of *raki* into his belt. Then he stepped onto the dance floor and spun around, his shoulders rounded and his arms stretched out in an arc before him.

The *zeimbekiko* is a strong, moody dance. The dancer tells tales: of friendship, of a proud manhood, of lost love. Kemal danced so well that Bill left the table and crouched beside the dance floor to clap him on. Dimitri got up too, and placed an empty shot glass at Kemal's feet; the idea was for Kemal to circle the glass and to dip low enough to fill it from his bottle of *raki* without using his hands – an ambitious manoeuvre, and Kemal, for all his skill, wasn't up to it.

And that was when the *kefi* soured. Dimitri tried to pull Bill upright, to force him to join Kemal. Bill refused; Dimitri insisted. Bill backed away, returning to sit with me. Dimitri and Kemal followed, Dimitri murmuring something about Bill's liver and how we weren't 'real' Greeks. They switched to Turkish, and Kemal laughed.

Dimitri leaned across the table and picked up Bill's packet of Marlboro. Bill ignored him. "Why were you laughing?" he asked Kemal.

Dimitri scowled and tossed the cigarettes back. "American cigarettes," he muttered. "Greeks don't smoke these."

Kemal had been looking away, across the empty dance floor. Turning back towards us he gave a self-deprecating smile. "We thought you were like Englishmen, you know. Not eating, not drinking . . ." And he gave an awkward shrug.

At the birthday table, champagne was popped and a giant, blazing cake was carried in for the six-year-old, who joined his father and the tireless foursome of ladies in a triumphant *tsifteteli*. The father, a handsome, mustachioed man, piled lire notes on top of his son's head. I tried not to look at Kemal and Dimitri, tried to forget what had just been said. Stavros was playing old standards; songs that I remembered from the Greek dinner dances I had attended as a teenager with my parents. The music flooded in: joyful, corny and familiar. I danced with the women again.

Stavros was winding up his set, playing a medley of faster and faster songs for his finale. Dimitri jack-knifed up to every woman in the room, starting with the younger, prettier ones, and ending with the lady with no neck. She was still smiling and shimmying: the evening's uncrowned *kefi* queen. They danced around each other, arms outstretched, wrists twirling, eyes shining. Dimitri moved closer to his partner and popped a piece of cheese into her mouth; she held his gaze, chewing the cheese in time to the music. "Yes," said her eyes. "What now? Is there more?" They danced in tighter and tighter circles, the woman's gaze controlling their movements and compelling the attention of the room. "Yes, yes, yes," her eyes said. "What else? Show me more."

Finally, Dimitri came to a standstill. He put his arms around the woman's waist, lifted her up and carried her around the floor. The spell was broken. The room erupted into laughter and applause as the song ended.

We stayed on until the restaurant closed. Kemal offered Stavros a lift home; on the way, Stavros told us with some pride that he had recently married under unusual circumstances. Perhaps he sensed that something had gone wrong, and meant his story to be a kind of peace offering. He told us that his wife had 'done the turn': that is, she had converted to Orthodoxy. She had been baptised and taken the Greek name of Eleni. It was rare for a Muslim woman to convert, Stavros said; usually the Greek man made the change in such marriages. His wife's case was atypical, however, because her family had once been Orthodox. They had converted to Islam after the Asia Minor Catastrophe; by turning back, she was not only claiming a husband, but reclaiming her family's lost Greekness. She was also helping Stavros fulfil a promise. Before his death, Stavros's father had asked him, as the only Christian left in the family, to keep his faith. But according to Stavros, his religious belief went deeper than a son's obligation to his father: he felt a strong, personal connection to the Greek Church. It was a powerful feeling, one that he was willing to describe but unable to explain. He simply believed that one day the Church would rise again and be great, and that the time was approaching.

><

Whenever one enters the church to pray, one understands immediately that it has been fashioned not by any human power but by the influence of God. And so the mind is lifted up to God and exalted, feeling that He cannot be far away but must love to dwell in this place which He has chosen.

That was what the historian Procopius wrote about the Church of the Divine Wisdom, Hagia Sophia, in 557, twenty years after the church was first dedicated. For the following millennium his assessment – that the supernatural had played a part in the building's construction – was implicitly shared by the Orthodox faithful, who believed that the church had no equal in all the world.

When Constantinople claimed that its civilisation was 'higher' – spiritually, artistically and practically – than all others, Hagia Sophia was its argument and proof. It was a gleaming, golden marvel with a soaring dome and mosaics that appeared to span the heavens. Technically unparalleled, it satisfied the intellect and overwhelmed the senses. Even today, stripped of much of its Christian context and filled with tourists, its great halls tell stories that can be heard in no other place.

When Constantinople finally fell, in 1453, all the people of the city gathered in Hagia Sophia to pray. According to legend, when the Turks entered the church, the priest performing the liturgy disappeared into its walls; he will emerge to continue his prayers when the city is returned to the Greeks.

The sack of the city, the desecration of the holy places, the rape and the slaughter, the looting and the wreckage passed into legend too. Critobulus, a Christian in the service of the conquering sultan, Mehmet II, wrote of his master that: 'When he saw the ravages, the destruction and the deserted houses and all that had perished and become ruins, then a great sadness took possession of him and he repented . . . Tears came to his eyes and sobbing he expressed his sadness. "What a town this was! And we have allowed it to be destroyed!" His soul was full of sorrow. And in truth it was natural, so much did the horror of the situation exceed all limits.'

Hagia Sophia was stripped of its jewel-studded ornaments, its icons and relics. The cathedral that had been the glory of the

Byzantine empire was turned into a mosque; its famous mosaics were plastered over. The building had always contained paradoxes: once it had expressed both imperial ambition and an unworldly harmony; now it became the chief trophy of a new empire and the most enduring symbol of what the Greeks had lost.

These days Hagia Sophia is a museum. It was our last stop in Istanbul: Bill said it was impossible to leave the city before we had paid our respects.

We walked around in golden shadows. Half of the great dome's interior was obscured by a tower of scaffolding and the galleries were filled with chattering tour groups. But despite them – even despite the bare, neglected look of its walls – the building slowly, imperceptibly, confounded us with its magic.

It is huge. A built sky swells up: it curves, shadows fall, and you enter a dark and regal realm. Works of art are always bound to the culture from which they come; artists are sometimes credited with transcending the world around them, but the best they can do is give it its highest expression. Nine hundred years before Hagia Sophia, the Athenians built the Parthenon. It also served the dual role of political boast and holy shrine; it too was dedicated to divine wisdom, in the form of the goddess Athena. When Greeks mourn the fate of Hagia Sophia they do more than rue the fall of Constantinople. They mourn their failure, so far, to build another place so perfectly beautiful that it becomes a parable deep and true enough to compel their gaze away from what they have left behind.

---

* A third exception was made for the Orthodox peoples living on the Turkish-controlled islands of Tenedos and Imroz at the mouth of the

Dardanelles. An open prison for criminals from continental Turkey was opened on Imroz; the Greek population of the island has fallen from 8000 in 1922 to 400 inhabitants today. The Greek population on Tenedos was 5320 in 1922, while today it is no more than 100. (Information from the Greek Ministry of Foreign Affairs.)

Chapter Seven

On the Plain

T HE OPENNESS OF Thrace is deceptive; its plains hold secrets. In the south, where Greek culture is mostly homogeneous, people speak of Thrace warily. To them, it is a land of fringe dwellers, of ethnic curiosities. The region's wide plains and immense, variegated skies have long accommodated difference: here, Greeks walk on hot coals, slender minarets grace the horizon, flamingoes migrate to the wetlands.

A friend of mine called John once told me about the time he had driven through Thrace, and had left the main road on a whim, prompted by the sight of a tall African and his family waiting for the local bus; they did not look like tourists. A side road led John directly to a village that was divided into two; one part housed a community of Greek-speaking Nubians. Intrigued, John stopped at the nearest *kafeneion*, where the Greek owner told him that Nubians had lived in the area for a long time. The *kafetzis* whistled through his teeth and made a scooping gesture with his hand when asked exactly how long: Greek shorthand for very long, for years beyond number. (In the characteristic Greek way, the *kafetzis* preferred the vague, expressive gesture to mundane fact.) John eventually learned that the Nubians had come to the region as the servants of an Ottoman governor, most likely one who had come from Egypt. Once released from their master's service, they had settled peacefully in Greece and had multiplied.

In the mountains of Thrace's Greek-Bulgarian border live the Pomaks, a separate ethnic group of practising Muslims, who, according to some sources, are able to trace their ancestry back to Alexander the Great (probably the north's most commonly claimed progenitor). The vexed question of their origins has degenerated into a self-interested political dispute: the Greeks, the Turks and the Bulgarians all claim the Pomaks as their own. It is said that they collaborated with the Bulgarians during the Bulgarian occupation of Thrace in the Second World War, in response to which the Greek Government made it illegal for the Pomaks to leave their home area without a permit. The condition was only waived in 1995.

Also in Thrace are Greeks who have returned from the Pontus (the Greek name for the Black Sea), which has been a site of Greek colonisation since ancient times. Many have left the Pontus since the collapse of Communism, and have been encouraged to settle in Thrace and neighbouring Macedonia. On my journey through Thrace I met a newly arrived Pontian, a self-effacing taxi driver with hesitant Greek. Originally from Odessa, he'd migrated to Greece with his wife and daughter; returning to Thrace was, for him, rather like a reunion with an estranged relative – his family had lived in the Pontus for 150 years.

He told me the following story. During the Stalin era, his father, a baker, had been stripped of his assets and exiled to Kazakhstan; like many Greeks, he had been targeted for persecution because of his relative wealth. After years of exile, the family returned to the Black Sea to start again. But that was not the end of their travails. After the collapse of the Soviet empire, the rise of ethnic consciousness in the region meant that the Greeks were once again unwelcome in the Pontus. The driver predicted that in a few years no Greeks would be left there. He threw up a hand and looked heavenward – the fatalistic gesture that means 'what can you do?'. He was not an ambitious man; he simply wanted to survive the arbitrariness of history.

Exile, identity and the prison of ethnicity. In Thrace different strands of Greekness rode the wind like so many migratory birds. When Bill and I stopped in Alexandroupolis en route to Istanbul, an old Pontian man had played us a song. He was sitting in the corner of a *kafeneion* weaving a plaintive tune on his fiddle. We knew he was a Pontian because of the way he held the instrument vertically against his chest; it is a style peculiar to the Pontus and to Crete. He played in the same ruminative spirit in which other people stare out to sea. His purpose was not to entertain; he was engaged in a private contemplation and was oblivious to his surroundings. People sitting close by affected not to notice the old man, but Bill and I were seated at an outside table near the door and we watched him obliquely. "There he goes again," remarked a passer-by. "Hear the old Pontian crying for his home."

><

Iasmos was a short bus ride away from the Thracian town of Komotini, where we had based ourselves for a few days. The village sat in the middle of a plain; mountains rose in the distance, and way behind them, on the other side of their wildness, lay Bulgaria. The anonymity of the eastern border, where the division between Greece and Turkey appeared to be no more than an arbitrary line, was behind us now, yet the countryside still lacked the drama that is typical of much of Greece.

Nazif Ferhat stood waiting for Bill and me at the Iasmos bus stop. He was a slight, dark-haired man with melancholy eyes, whose greeting was softly spoken but unselfconscious. Within just a few moments he had quietly put us at our ease, and the awkwardness that often comes when talking to a stranger in an unfamiliar place passed without our noticing.

Like Iasmos itself, Nazif's apartment was smaller and more unassuming than I had expected. Nazif was a dentist, and his wife, Nermin, was a bright-eyed, handsome woman who had trained as a lawyer; the couple had met and fallen in love while they were both students at the University of Istanbul. Despite their professional credentials, the family lived modestly. Although Nermin did not look the part of a provincial housewife, that is what she had become; over tea, she told us that she had never practised law because her Greek was not good enough and, besides, she had children to raise. Nazif's Greek, by contrast, was fluent and easy. He had not attended the Turkish schools favoured by most members of his community, but had gone to Greek schools instead, as did their two children. While we spoke, their daughter, a shy beauty of about ten, sat nearby, alert and silent.

I had been asked to contact Nazif by Fedai Ali, who had grown up next door to him in Iasmos. Fedai, his wife, Suheyeli, and their son lived in Melbourne now. Migration had brought them material ease, but prosperity had not erased their feelings of displacement. So in 1991, after five years in Australia, they tried to go back to Thrace. They sold their house and business and flew home, only to be told at Athens airport that their Greek citizenship had been taken from them: returning was impossible.

Fedai had told me this story in his brick-veneer home in outer-suburban Melbourne. We spoke in Greek, our shared second language. He had a youthful, even jaunty appearance; the blow that regional politics had dealt him had not extinguished his energy and optimism. As we spoke, Suheyeli, a slender, fair-haired woman in jeans, sat in the corner of the room, smoking anxiously. Mostly her days were spent in the clothing factory the Alis owned, where she worked with other Turks; but their company could not replace the effortless sense of belonging that came with village life. Suheyeli's eyes filled with tears. "I want to live near my sisters," she said. "I want to see my mother again."

Fedai showed me his Australian passport with its stamp denying him entry back into Greece. He had lost his citizenship under the Greek Nationality Law of 1955, in which a person of 'non-Greek origin leaving Greece without the intention of returning may be declared as having lost Greek nationality'.* Fedai had placed the matter in the hands of a Greek lawyer in Komotini, who told him that the loss of citizenship was the most significant human rights issue facing the Muslims of Thrace; he knew of more than 400 cases in the Rodopi region alone.

><

Nazif was well versed in the twists and turns of Fedai's story. Drily, he remarked that his friend had been punished for wanting to make money and for leaving his home. But Nazif too had left Iasmos, in order to study in Istanbul after failing to gain a place at the University of Thessaloniki. He felt no particular loyalty to the Turkish city, visiting it only under sufferance.

We spent the afternoon with Nazif in our stockinged feet – our shoes having been left at the door – drinking tea and mulling over the political and cultural complexities that bedevil this part of the world.

According to Nazif, the position of the Thracian Turks deteriorated sharply after the military junta came to power in 1967. "It was obvious that the Government wanted us to leave. And we have gone – to Turkey, to Germany and even to Australia." The number of Turks living in Thrace – about 120,000 – has remained steady since the community was protected by the Treaty of Lausanne in 1923. But in the years since the treaty, the ethnic profile of the region has changed: the Muslims who once dominated Thrace are now a minority. Complaints that Greek policies have not allowed the Thracian Turks to experience a natural rate of increase fail to gain much sympathy in Greece, however; the near disappearance of the Greeks in Istanbul, a community that was also protected by the treaty, is generally cited to prove that not only have the Greeks suffered more, they are also a more generous people.

"It is certain that the Greeks in Istanbul have had a worse time than us," said Nazif mildly, "but it's a silly parallel. One shouldn't compare the two communities. I want to be compared with my neighbours in Greece, not with the Greeks in Istanbul."

During the junta years, members of the Turkish community lost the right to buy land, to hold a driver's licence or even to repair their own houses, rights that were restored by the Papandreou Government. While acknowledging that gains have been made, the community still feels thwarted; small but symbolically important impediments remain.[†]

In discussing such matters, Nazif appeared to be genuinely free of hatred; nor did he assume any malice or prejudice on our part. He had no interest in point scoring, or in casting himself as a victim of Greek chauvinism. Bill and I had already spent two long days in Komotini talking to community leaders and politicians. After having to sit through hours of complaint, pomposity and pontification, we both found it a great relief to speak to someone like Nazif.

"I think we've spent too much time here talking to politicians," I remarked.

"Maybe. But I am also a politician."

At this, Nazif's daughter broke her silence with an infectious snort of laughter. We looked at her questioningly.

"What's so funny?" asked her father.

"How can you be a politician when no-one votes for you?" she answered.

Nazif tried, unsuccessfully, to curb her cheekiness with a stern look. He explained that he was the local candidate for Synaspismos, a democratic offshoot of the Communist Party.[‡] It was true, he conceded, that he had so far attracted very few votes. He continued to stand because he believed that the mainstream parties could not be trusted. They played politics with the ethnic vote and appeared to have no real interest in helping the people of Thrace. Greeks and Turks – they were used to living together; if left alone, they would muddle along well enough. We had heard this before, but most people's tolerance contained an element of self-congratulation; they made a small parade of their

157

enlightened attitude, whereas Nazif's words were suffused with an undercurrent of melancholy.

"Our problems are not difficult to solve," he concluded, "it's just that no-one has the will to do it."

Before we left Iasmos, we walked through the village to visit Fedai Ali's parents. The streets were strewn with cotton balls that had fallen from trucks carrying the harvest from the nearby cotton fields. An open-air market was breaking up; a Turkish woman in a headscarf caught our eye and held a bag of apples aloft. A chattering procession of Muslim women dressed in traditional black scarves and coats were on their way to an engagement ceremony. They talked briefly with Nazif's wife – their pretty faces at odds with the drabness of their clothes – before continuing on their way.

Fedai's parents lived in a double-storey stone house behind a high wall. The gate was opened by Mr Ali: a small, alert man dressed in work pants and a knitted black beanie. His Greek was poor, but peppered with slangy idiomatic phrases such as one might hear bandied about in a *kafeneion*; he was a builder by trade. His wife's eyes grew wet with tears when she saw me, an emissary from the distant land that held her son. The old lady conveyed her gratitude for our visit by serving us coffee in tiny cups and sprinkling eau de Cologne into our palms. She could not speak a word of Greek, although she had spent all her life in Greece – many more years than my father the patriot. Mrs Ali lived in a world utterly isolated from the Greekness that was so central to my father's sense of self.

I told the old couple what I could about Fedai, but it didn't amount to very much.

"And what work does my son do in Australia?" asked Mr Ali.

I looked at Nazif in puzzlement. "He knows," Nazif told me

softly. "He just wants to hear it from you."

"He owns a clothing factory," I said. And sure enough, on hearing these words, Mr Ali beamed a proud smile of satisfaction.

Before we left, the old man asked if he could look at my passport. It was an Australian passport like his son's. He riffled through the pages, staring at the stamps without expression, before handing it back.

"Have you ever had a problem with this?" he asked.

For a moment I wondered if he supposed that the difficulty surrounding Fedai's re-entry into Greece lay in some detectable flaw in his travel documents – the colour of the ink, or the size of the print perhaps – rather than in the troubled history of Turkish and Greek relations.

The old man's ingenuous query triggered a wave of shame, but I endeavoured not to show it. "No," I said. "I have never had any problems at all."

><

Nazif drove us back to Komotini, full of apologies for the shabbiness of his car. On the way, he pointed out the river where he and Fedai had gone fishing together and the neighbouring village where his wife had been born. The late afternoon sky was enormous, the clouds billowing impressively as though to compensate for the meandering flatness of the plain, the bewildering sameness of the fields.

As we approached the town, Nazif quietly remarked: "A white car has been following us for a while. It is probably the police."

Bill and I looked behind us in alarm. Neither of us had noticed the small white car. As Nazif double-parked in the square outside our hotel, the white car pulled up behind us. Nazif said he had first noticed it when we had driven by his wife's village; it was therefore possible that the police had been discreetly monitoring our movements all afternoon. Bill and I stared in disbelief as two casually dressed men got out of the car and sauntered towards a kiosk on the corner of the square. Then the driver of the white car pulled away.

"They just want to scare you," said Nazif.

"Well, they've succeeded."

Nazif allowed himself a small smile at our expense. "You don't have anything to worry about," he said. "The worst they can do is take you to the station for questioning."

It was hardly a comforting remark, but Nazif's intentions were good. We thanked him, and he told us to phone if we needed any help. Then he too drove away.

Our first impulse was to check our hotel room to see if it had been searched in our absence. It appeared to be untouched. Before we went out again, however, I took two snapshots of my son from a folder in my case and put them in my wallet; I had a superstitious dread of strangers handling the photographs. As we walked back through the lobby I saw one of the men from the white car leaving the hotel. I remembered an odd occurrence that had taken place the day before, when we were lunching at a small restaurant near the centre of Komotini. Halfway through our meal, the waiter had asked me if my name was Katerina: I was wanted on the telephone. I'd felt a small jolt of fear. None of our acquaintances knew our whereabouts. "Maybe we are being followed," I'd joked to Bill. But as it turned out, the caller was chasing someone else with same name. We'd chuckled at the coincidence and he'd apologised for disturbing me.

"*Koppelia* – Girlie!" The hotel receptionist, a woman of my own age with peroxided hair and an annoyingly patronising manner, was calling me. Did I have ID?

"Why do you want it? We already showed our ID when we checked in."

"We have his ID," – and here she nodded towards Bill – "but we haven't seen yours."

"But that's not unusual, is it? Usually one ID is enough."

She didn't answer but held out her hand for the passport. Irritated, I waited as she took down my particulars. What was this about? Had someone asked her for my ID? I guessed that she wouldn't answer my questions, so I didn't ask them.

When the receptionist had finished, Bill and I walked across the square to a cafe and ordered a pizza. It was late afternoon; we hadn't eaten a proper meal since breakfast. The restaurant was decorated in a flash modern style to attract moneyed students from the university; rock and roll thudded out with a dull inevitability. We went upstairs to escape the noise and sat near the window, looking down at the two men from the white car as they paced up and down. Occasionally they looked back up at us.

"This is ridiculous," said Bill. "These guys are so obvious."

"Well, if the idea is to scare us, it's their job to be obvious."

Bill told me of a cousin of ours, now a magistrate, who had been followed by the police while she was a law student in Komotini. The reason, she believed, was that she had befriended some Turkish students. We supposed that we had attracted attention by visiting Ismail Rodoplu, a Turk who had represented Thrace in the Greek Parliament. We had talked to Rodoplu – a hearty, red-haired fellow – in his office that morning. The scene had recalled the smoky, conspiratorial atmosphere of a village *kafeneion*, with its perpetual crowd of gossips, intriguers and hangers-on. A boy was summoned to fetch a tray loaded with coffee and iced water from a nearby shop; meanwhile a knot of Turkish men walked in and out of the office, whispering, listening, drinking coffee and occasionally joining in. A Turkish lawyer interrupted from time to time to clear up ambiguities in Rodoplu's Greek. Rodoplu was concerned that no Turks had been compensated for damages incurred during the Komotini riots of 1990, when a Greek crowd had smashed and looted Turkish shops and businesses, including his electoral office. Apparently, only a small proportion of the Turks affected had filed for compensation; they were too frightened to make a legal protest and had little confidence in the system.

Our pizza arrived: vegetarian with chilli. I picked up a piece and peered down at the men from the white car. They were smoking and looking bored. I thought about how terrible I would feel if this surveillance led to a stamp in my passport denying me entry back into Greece, and I asked Bill to ring our cousin the magistrate for advice. She told him not to worry: she did not believe the police would search our room, or even call us in for questioning. We had done nothing wrong. "They just want to scare you," she said.

"This really isn't so bad," said Bill, putting away his mobile phone. "It's all good material. After this I'll be able to write about what it feels like to be followed. I might include a little episode like this in my next book."

"And how do you feel? What will you say?"

He thought about it for a moment and looked down again at the two men in the square. "That it makes you paranoid – but if you eat a pizza you feel better."

That evening we went to the movies and saw an execrable

action film involving fast cars, gun fights, explosions, mistaken identity and a vegetarian girl in a mini-skirt. When we returned to our hotel room the phone was ringing. I picked up the receiver, but no-one was there.

≥⋖

An army band woke us early the next morning, our last in Komotini. It was rehearsing the national anthem for the Ohi (or 'No') march that was to take place in every main street in Greece later that day. I stepped onto our balcony, with its Arabian Nights view of a minaret silhouetted against the distant hills, and glanced down at the soldiers. They looked rather comical, like khaki-coloured wind-up toys. Their routine involved turning corners, apparently at random, while blowing bugles and banging drums. I wondered out loud if we would arrive at Xanthi – our next stop – in time for the march. Bill made a dry remark about the noisy intrusion of ill-timed nationalism; hadn't I seen enough of that already? He was opposed, on principle, to all patriotic display.

Before checking out we breakfasted at a modest little *bougatsa* shop on the other side of the square. As far as possible, I was following a *bougatsa*-a-day policy while in northern Greece. The best places were unpretentious, with lino floors and steamy windows; they only served three or four varieties of the filo-pastry pies (custard, cheese, spinach and mince were the standards), and were open early in the morning. Many did not have chairs or tables; you took the *bougatsa* away, wrapped up in paper, or maybe ate it standing at the counter. On this morning, Bill bought an extra one for an Albanian child whom we had seen every day, begging for coins. The woman in the shop smiled at Bill but glared at the child; she didn't want him hanging around. The dark-haired boy was dressed in clothes that were too thin, and his face was unwashed. He murmured thanks, grabbed the slightly greasy parcel and ran away.

We saw illegal refugees from Albania's collapsed Hoxha regime in every town through which we passed. They were, for the most part, beggars and scapegoats, accused of petty theft and of making the streets unsafe: a real indictment in a country that has always prided itself on the civility of its urban life. On a social level, Albanians were barely tolerated. Complaints about their shiftlessness were as common as conversations about the weather. But they were also widely employed as casual labourers because they would work for half the daily rate paid to Greeks. It was an inconsistency that few Greeks were prepared to acknowledge.

"*Kaki anthropi*," said the woman in the *bougatsa* shop, gesturing towards the fleeing boy. "Bad people."

"This place is full of people who don't like each other," said Bill as we walked back to the hotel. He offered to bring our bags down to the foyer while I settled the bill. The bottle blonde was at the desk again. Without looking up, she charged me 2500 drachmas more for the room than we had negotiated.

"You've made a mistake," I said.

"Maybe you just didn't understand my girl."

"I don't think so . . ."

Bill arrived with the bags. He was the one who had arranged the price for the room, so I explained the problem to him. The blonde was now openly agitated. She asked him to describe the receptionist he had dealt with.

Bill shrugged. "It was a man . . ."

"That's impossible. No man was working when you checked in. You're lying. That's the second lie you've told me."

Her raised voice was filled with hatred. The conflict over the bill was merely the hook for her anger, not its underlying cause.

Bill picked up our bags and cocked his head towards the door. "Let's get out of here."

A man emerged from the office behind the desk. Steadily, quietly, he told the receptionist to accept the price Bill had agreed to pay. Relieved by his intervention, I counted out the drachma notes. Nobody spoke. But as we walked through the door, the blonde was unable to resist shouting a final farewell: "You'll be arrested one day!"

><

Talk and cigarette smoke billowed over the chairs and tables of Xanthi's Plateia Eleftherias, or Freedom Square, the mixture of boredom and self-importance peculiar to parade days having metamorphosed into a cosy garrulousness. Stragglers from the Ohi parade were still spilling in from 28 October Street, named for the very date the people were celebrating. Everybody had dressed for the occasion: fathers in suits; mothers in well-cut coats and patent-leather shoes; teenagers turned out like the flag in blue-and-white school uniforms; conscripts in jungle greens; children in tasselled hats and waistcoats sumptuously embroidered in red and gold. Bill, who had complained of a headache during the march, had livened up, cheered by the crowd. The small pleasures of the national holiday – dressing up, showing off one's children, talking to one's neighbours – that was the type of patriotism he understood.

165

The Ohi march celebrates the day in 1940 when Prime Minister Ioannis Metaxas said "No" to the Italian invasion. Metaxas was an unpopular leader who headed a police state, but by refusing to give in to Mussolini he transcended his limitations and expressed his people's determination to fight for their independence. In doing so, he provided the country with a moment of triumph in what was to become a tragically divisive conflict.

Xanthi is two cities in one: the prosperous modern town sprawls along a plain, while the old quarter leans against the foothills of the Rodopi mountain range and climbs upward. The old joins the new in a jumble of tavernas, *ouzeria* and wine bars in the ever-narrowing streets near the square. Beguiled, Bill and I strolled past crumbling nineteenth-century mansions built on exhaled tobacco fortunes, and admired the Turkish-style houses, their elaborately strutted wooden balconies overhanging the lanes. We could tell which houses had Turkish-speaking occupants because of the satellite dishes – for Turkish television – perched on their roofs.

We walked uphill until we reached the end of the old town. Here, like an unexpected gift, was the scent of pines and the uncompromising face of the mountains. A fine rain was falling, making the smell of the earth and the trees more pungent; I felt a rush of happiness, accompanied by nostalgia for my father's village.

Clanging bells drew our attention to a flock of goats on the meandering road above us, and as we looked up, the black of a shepherd's cloak flashed through the foliage. I hoped it belonged to a Sarakatsan – a tribe of shepherds and nomads, many of whom had settled in Thrace. But as soon as we spotted him, the shepherd left the road and deftly picked his way along a path that wound through the forest. We watched until the last members of his flock clambered up the slope behind him, leaving clots of mud in their wake. A downpour was threatening, but neither of us wanted to go back. We stood on the crest of the town, breathing in the fragrant air and listening to the fading sound of the bells. It was a relief to have left the crowd, even for a short time, and to be in sight of the high country again.

><

"Let me tell you straight: the Sarakatsans today are no different from you and me. They live in houses and pay taxes and catch the bus to work. They have nothing that distinguishes them from ordinary Greeks."

Thanassi was exasperated. He was a high school teacher in Xanthi and the first cousin of my *koumbara* – the dear friend in Melbourne who was my son's godmother. Traditionally, the *koumbara* relationship is as strong as a blood tie, and Thanassi felt obliged, on behalf of his Australian relative, to show me whatever hospitality he could. So he forced himself to leave his fiancée's side on a Sunday and set out with Bill and me in search of Sarakatsans. He placed himself at our service for the whole day: on the one hand making generous suggestions about where more Sarakatsans could be found, and on the other gruffly exclaiming that the business of searching out such people was a misguided folly.

Though I was loath to admit it, Thanassi's impatience with the exercise had some justification. He was quite right: I did harbour dreamy notions about the Sarakatsans. But how could it be otherwise? Everything I knew about the shepherds was pure romance.[§]

167

For centuries – or perhaps aeons, for much of their history is undocumented and their origins are obscure – the Sarakatsans had lived as wanderers. The other nomadic shepherds of Greece, such as the Vlachs of Epiros (with whom the Sarakatsans, to their chagrin, are sometimes confused), were actually semi-nomadic, settling for the winter and following their flocks over the mountains in the warmer months. The Sarakatsans, however, were true nomads. The roof of the Balkans was their home: all of it and none of it. They had grazed their flocks on the peaks of Epiros, Albania, Macedonia, Bulgaria and Western Turkey. Literally – and to my mind metaphorically – they had set themselves above the region's ethnic politics and territorial disputes. A proud people, they'd kept to themselves, believing their way of life to be superior to the lot of the villager, whose days were spent tending a small patch of land. But in the years following the Greek civil war, the shepherds left the high ground; with the Greek Government's encouragement, many gave up their wanderings to dwell on the sober plains of Thrace.

Only a generation had gone by since the Sarakatsans had abandoned their old ways, but if Thanassi was to be believed, whatever it was that had set the nomads apart (and he doubted whether it had ever amounted to very much) had long vanished. I wasn't convinced that he was right. Two days earlier I had spotted an old Sarakatsan woman on the Komotini-Xanthi bus, a faded blue cross tattooed on her forehead. Maybe that detail alone accounted for her air of separateness; maybe the circle of stillness surrounding her was conjured up by my own fancy. Later I learned that the cross had most likely been tattooed by her family during the days of the Turkish occupation; if the Turks kidnapped the child – and such practices were not unknown – she would be unable to forget her Christian origins.

Despite his misgivings, Thanassi took us to meet a Sarakatsan he knew of who worked in his neighbourhood. Stelios was a broad-shouldered florist, as handsome as a young Elvis. He sat surrounded by dried floral arrangements and pots bound with velvet ribbons; by his side was a textbook on the Greek-Italian campaign that he had been reading over his morning coffee. Stelios was flattered by my interest in his people, but also distracted by his need to arrange the morning's deliveries. He kept interrupting our conversation to take armfuls of flowers to a van outside.

What did it mean to be a Sarakatsan? For Stelios, a childhood in which his father had been unable to support him, culturally or financially, because his flock – and a large part of his identity – had disappeared during the war. Like most Sarakatsans, his father had been illiterate. He had been conscripted in 1939 and had served for eight years and eight months, fighting first on the Albanian front against the Italians (Stelios had been reading about the stories his father had told him in the history book by his side) and later against the left-wing guerrillas in the Greek civil war.

It was the war, you see, the bloody civil war, that had killed the nomadic life, Stelios said. The guerrillas had stolen their flocks for food; because the rebels were desperate and hungry, but also because so many of the shepherds were soldiers on the Government side. "But in my father's case, he had no choice in the matter, this was not a fate he asked for, he was not an educated man." In any event, it was fear of the guerrillas that first sent the nomads to dwell on the plain.

For his own part, Stelios had never known the nomadic life and so had no particular feeling for it. Also, not everything about his people's past was good. Their nomadic society had been strict

169

and hierarchical; the leader was the *tsellingas*, the richest and most powerful man in the group, and sometimes the only literate one. Stelios's father, on the other hand, had belonged to the lowest caste; when he came back from the war, he'd had to work for a *tsellingas* because he no longer had a flock of his own.

Stelios pulled a wry face; he did not miss the old feudal distinctions and the humiliations that had come with them. But all the same, there was a great deal that he valued in his family's heritage. He had married a Sarakatsan woman; he believed the Sarakatsans had better morals than other Greeks, no offence to the present company intended.

His father was dead now and his mother, well, she had a sadness inside her that time had not healed. Not that she complained; that was not her way. But once a year, during the Feast of the Prophet Elijah, the family travelled to the mountains again (chapels to the prophet, like ancient temples of Apollo, are always found in elevated spots), and whenever their car passed a certain point on the road – a stand of pines that indicated they were truly in the mountains once more – his mother would weep for the life she had lost.

After we had left Stelios in his cave of roses, Thanassi gave full vent to his scepticism. "What he didn't tell you is that the Sarakatsans were fascists," he said. "And their women never stopped working. That is what the traditional way of life meant – hardship, poverty and work that never ended."

Bill rolled his eyes. He had no particular interest in the Sarakatsans but found their company preferable to Thanassi's dogmatic pronouncements. He spent the day smoking and looking sceptically upon the proceedings.

And gentle Antonia gave no indication that she believed she had been hard done by. She lived with her family in a double-storey house on the outskirts of Xanthi.

"*Ai ai*," she cried, when Thanassi introduced us. "If I'd known you were coming, I would have made a lovely pie, a lovely cheese pie like I made when I was a girl." Although she was only sixty, her thin, frail body and delicate, lined skin gave her the appearance of an old, old lady.

When she realised that I was interested in the old way of life, Antonia rummaged in her cupboards and brought out a battered circular pie dish, the same one she had used over campfires as a young woman.

"We would roll out the pastry with a long stick like this," – and here she pointed to a broom handle – "and then we would bake the pies on top of the fire. We always had cheese and milk and yoghurt from the sheep, you see. I can make you the most delicious pies you ever tasted."

Antonia bustled around and poured us each a glass of home-made wild-cherry brandy, calculating aloud how long it would take to make a roll of pastry if she dropped everything and started right away. She told us that when her family finally settled in 1960, life became harder, with more worries and less joy. When she was a girl, all the women would work together – spinning or weaving or cooking, and singing all the while. Their skin was clear and glowing, they had rosy cheeks and red lips because of the exercise, the wholesome food and the clean air. When the time came to have a baby – well, you just squatted down and out it came. The midwife would cut the cord and wrap the baby up and the mother would carry on with her work. Nobody got sick or complained, it was a natural thing. Now, well ... the one good thing was that the men didn't go away any more. Once, they used to leave for the high pastures for months on end, but now – thanks be to God – families were together all the time. Family life and

171

love: they were the great, the important things. That was what we had to hold on to.

When we finally said goodbye, Antonia was standing under a tree in her garden, waving and smiling. "Next time you come, give me some warning," she called out. "I want to make you a wonderful pie."

We met other Sarakatsans that day. Some of them were still shepherds, but none of them were nomads. Antonia was the only Sarakatsan I met who had actually lived the old life; all the others only had second-hand memories of it. They were bemused by my interest in them, and when I asked a group of men where they thought the Sarakatsans had originally come from, they began to laugh.

"You tell us," said a handsome farmer, his leathery, tanned face creased with a knowing smile.

"I don't know."

"Well, who do we look like?"

He gave me a penetrating look, but I had no idea what he was getting at. I shook my head.

"My girl, haven't you noticed? We look like you," and he gestured at Bill and me.

Everybody laughed again, and so did I. It was true. These men, indeed all the Sarakatsans I met that day, were strikingly similar in appearance to the people in my father's village. Most were tall and rangy, many had high cheekbones and some were fair-skinned and blue-eyed.

A penchant for physiological detective work is common in Greece, and may be connected to the country's dearth of ancestral records. Genealogical book-keeping was largely unknown during the Turkish occupation, leaving a hole in people's knowledge about their origins. So Greeks turn to their bodies for clues about who they are: for instance, a flat back of the head is thought to be an Epirot characteristic, while high cheekbones are said to indicate a connection with the invading Bulgar tribes of old. Greek looks are far from uniform. Thanassi's short, squat and bald-headed appearance, for example, was utterly different from that of the still-laughing Sarakatsans.

The idea that there was a link between these northern nomads and the mountain-dwellers of the Peloponnese was intriguing. Even though I knew that the connection was, in all likelihood, illusory, I was nevertheless delighted to discover even a tenuous tie between myself and these enigmatic mountain-wanderers. It satisfied a hunger; the same hunger that was shared by all the disparate peoples of Thrace. And wasn't curiosity about that hunger – and the dark intolerance that it bred – the reason I had come to the north? The Turks, the Pomaks, the Pontians, the Jews of Thessaloniki, the Slavic-speakers of Macedonia and the Albanians of southern Epiros – the north was full of their separate pasts, their griefs, and their competing claims on Greek history. But the longer I stayed among them, the stronger grew my wish to head for the hills. I wanted to clear my mind of the tangle of politics and border skirmishes, to feel untrammelled again, to step over the land as lightly as an old Sarakatsan.

It was time to stop moving around, time to go back. Bill had a road movie to write, and I needed to return to my family and to the stories that were waiting in the mountains of Chrysambela.

* The Minister for Macedonia-Thrace, Mr Philippos Petsalnikos, told me that the practice of withdrawing nationality has been discontinued.

For ethnic Greeks, however, Greek citizenship can be notoriously hard to lose. An emigrant returning to Greece for a holiday after three decades of working and paying taxes abroad can find himself called up for Greek national service after a three-month stay; so can his foreign-born son.

† A teacher from Komotini told me that the Turkish Teacher's Association had been forced to change its name to the Muslim Teacher's Association; the teachers – Greek citizens who were ethnically Turkish – were not allowed to describe themselves as Turkish. Rather than change its name, the outraged teachers disbanded the group.

The question of self-identification has become a highly charged political issue in Thrace. In January 1990, two Turkish political candidates for the Greek Parliament, the late Dr Sadik Ahmet and Mr Ismail Serif, received eighteen-month prison sentences for using the word 'Turkish' to describe their community (they served sixty-four days in a Thessaloniki prison and then were ordered to pay fines). Two days after the trial, a mob of Greeks rioted in Komotini.

‡ At the last election, the major parties fielded Muslim candidates: PASOK, New Democracy and Synaspismos each have a Muslim representative in Parliament.

§ I am indebted to Patrick Leigh Fermor's essay on the Sarakatsans, 'The Black Departers', in his book *Roumeli*.

PART THREE

THE VILLAGE

Under the plane tree, near the water, among the laurels,
sleep moved you about and scattered you
round me, near me, though I was not able to touch the whole
  of you,
joined as you were with your silence;
watching your shadow grow and dwindle,
lose itself among other shadows, in that
other world that was holding and letting you go.

from 'Sleep', by George Seferis

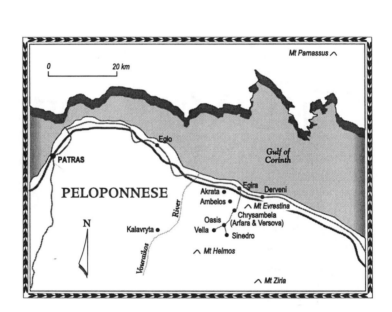

CHAPTER EIGHT

CHRYSAMBELA

BEARINGS

L ANDSCAPES ARE LIKE other people's faces: familiarity changes how we see them, and so does our inner view, the climate behind the eyes. Sometimes I try to remember what a certain friend looked like the first time I saw her: frailer, less pretty, the sassiness betrayed by an unconscious downward turn in the corner of her mouth. In that glance, I saw both more and less than I realised. So it is with one's surroundings. When you first step into a landscape, you are also part of the scene, invisible only to yourself; when the view changes, so can you.

Chrysambela is built on a mountainside, about fifteen kilometres along a winding road that begins at Egira on the Gulf of Corinth. The road tells a story. On its lower reaches, near the sea, it climbs past orange and lemon groves, tavernas, shops and fancy, new cement houses. The trees change as the road climbs into a colder climate: hardy olives, interspersed with grapevines and occasional clusters of cypress, their dark fingers pointing to the sky. The snow line begins just below the village itself, marked by plane trees, pines, cherries and walnuts. The cherry trees are planted in neat rows between the houses; in winter, when their branches are bare, the village looks oddly transparent, dwellings and strings of washing appearing where once was an impenetrable wall of leaves.

Chrysambela is an invention. The settlement is really two separate villages – Arfara and Versova – that have merged as their people have left. As you approach, the road forks; the upper road leads directly to Arfara, with its separate square and church. My father's house stands at the midway point, and although both forks take us there, we prefer the high road. It passes a vine-covered hill called the Saracen's Mount, for reasons that have long been forgotten, and a chapel shrouded in cypresses. By the chapel stands a tree, an old oak; there's a wooden spout near the base of its trunk from which spring water pours in a modest stream, cold and steady. People say the oak is old because of its great size, but the tree has the strength and vigour of a man in his prime; it is still growing.

When Uncle Apostoli drove me to my father's house, he stopped the car so I could drink from the spring and look out over the vines towards the gulf. The oak appeared unaffected by the years that had passed since I last saw it. I climbed back into the car reassured; the oak was mighty still.

In this country, in all directions, the scenery changes; the land rises and falls like the sea. For the most part, the olive groves and vineyards around the village are planted in the steep valleys that surround it. The valleys, in turn, are fissured with their own hillocks, creeks and dales. Once, every scrap of land was farmed – even the scrubbiest, rockiest slope was put to some use – but now the days of self-sufficiency are over and cultivation is a struggle for the old folk who remain. Well-tended olive trees stand next to groves that are choked with nettles, as sad as haunted houses.

To know the land, you must know the stories contained within it; they bend our mood, change how and what we see. A clump of rocks marks the spot where Dimitra's dowry begins; a fig tree heralds the fields where Grandfather Vassili saved an inheritance by planting wild olives. The farmers have given the fields names; each has its own character, its own memories. Above the village are plains which, not so long ago, were sown with wheat; for the most part, they are hidden from view. A steep climb is rewarded by a pause in the upward folds of the land and the revelation of a long, flat place where the wind bends the grass. But the disused fields are rarely visited. Their stories have blown away.

Behind Arfara more mountains rise, higher and higher, stretching all the way to Arcadia. They look like a wall, with the rest of Greece hidden behind them. Roads and villages lurk within their creases, but the further you go, the fewer people you find. Prosperity has emptied the mountains, just as it has filled the strip of land along the coast with supermarkets, cement suburbs and a highway to Athens. Some shepherds remain, however, in the cold and solitary country at the top of the Peloponnese. From Chrysambela you can sometimes see them, roaming with their flocks among the chestnuts, the stunted cedars and the thorny, wild pears of the high plains.

A triangle of mythological peaks frames Chrysambela. To the south-west is Helmos, source of the River Styx, where Thetis dipped her baby son Achilles in the waters of immortality, save for the heel by which she held him. To the south-east is Ziria, home of the Pleiades, the daughters of Atlas, before they became a fixture of the night sky. On the opposite side of the gulf is the apex, Mt Parnassus, sacred to Dionysos and Apollo; I could see it from our balcony. But very often, this northern aspect was invisible: land and sea would be swallowed by a milky haze. Sighting Parnassus became a private way of gauging how my luck was running: if by mid-morning the Sanctuary of Apollo had emerged from the blue, I took it as a sign that I was in for a good day.

The landscape's most defining feature, however, is the humble and largely unsung mountain of Evrestina. From the village, it often looked close enough to touch, but reaching its slopes was an arduous business: down a steep valley, over a creek and up again on the other side. A great-uncle of mine once owned a mill on its lower reaches, by a stream near a village called Monastiri. Grandfather Vassili used to walk there to grind the family's wheat, with a donkey to help carry the grain. The journey to the mill, the task of grinding and the walk back home was a long day's work.

Evrestina is a massive wall of ochre rock, whose colour deepens as the day wears on; come twilight, it fills the eastern sky with a rich orange hue. During the autumn, the moon too takes on an orange glow when it rises behind the mountain. When night has fallen, Evrestina fades to an inky shadow and Monastiri appears as a wavy line of lights, suspended in mid-air.

><

My father's house is on the outskirts of Versova, close to the fields that border the village; my parents, who were also spending some time in Greece, were living there with me. The day after I arrived, I went for a walk along the path that winds past the village school and through a cherry orchard, where mint and wild lavender grow in the shade. At the edge of the tree line, a rock rises out of the earth and leans over a precipice. Tiny clumps of cyclamen cling, limpet-like, in its shady hollows, and an irrigation channel that carries water from a nearby spring passes behind it. The view over the valley and to Evrestina on the other side emerges from the trees: a deep space filled with the valley's warm breath. In the spring, swallows ride the updraughts here, and in late autumn broad leaves from the plane trees that line the creek below rise up like balloons and fade into the sky.

It was siesta time. I sat in the sun for a while, looking about me. Although there were signs of human habitation all around – a vegetable plot, a line of trees, a track – the freedom and wildness of the place rang out like a song. The valley was invisible from the road, and this added to my pleasure: I could imagine that the scene belonged to me alone. Most of the villagers did not like to be away from these mountains for too long, but the reasons they gave were never aesthetic: they missed their neighbours, they said, or the water, or the air. The landscape was a given, like their hands and feet; rapturous appreciation was not required.

Two deserted monasteries look out over the edge of the valley. One, dedicated to the Virgin, stands next to the church on the outskirts of Monastiri; from my rock, I could see the dense thicket of cypress that marks the spot. The church is 600 years old and guards a miracle-working icon which, according to legend, was discovered under a slab of marble at the entrance to the church by a local woman who saw it in a dream. (In all likelihood, the marble had once been part of an ancient temple. According to the Greek historian Pausanias, Artemis was worshipped in these hills.) These days the icon is kept in a safe, but the priest – the son of the mill owner whom my grandfather used to visit – once brought it out for me to see. All that remained was a dark rectangle of wood, from which the paint had long faded. The priest, a slight, bright-eyed man, told me that the icon was indeed miraculous, and not simply because it had the power to answer prayers: the shadow of the Virgin and child was still imprinted on the wood. He held the icon to the light and I tried to make out the Holy Mother's outline on the dark, grainy surface; I thought I saw something, but couldn't be sure. The attempt to glimpse a shadow of an image was like a metaphor for faith itself.

The other monastery, Agios Vassili, is a humbler place. It isn't really a monastery at all, just two hermit cells built into the side of a hill. In the past, the villagers celebrated the Feast of Agios Vassilios – New Year's Day – by climbing up to the cells, listening to the liturgy and then picnicking on a little plain directly above.

The cells were only a short walk from my lookout rock; on an impulse, I decided to go there. I followed the irrigation channel along a ledge, past clusters of wild broom and feathery valerian. An old shepherd would often sit below the ledge, singing in the sunshine to his flock, but on this afternoon all was quiet. The channel leads to a copse of plane trees at the source of the spring, a place called Keneza. Even on the hottest days, the spring water is cold, and the air under the trees cool and sweet.

A steeply zigzagging line of cypress marked the path to Agios Vassili; it was a short, hard climb. Two Albanian boys were rumoured to be camping in the cells. Albanians had been wandering up to the village on foot, looking for work, ever since the collapse of Communism. At first they had been treated with suspicious contempt, but this had been replaced, over the years, with a wary tolerance. Poor Albanians were not too proud to work in the fields; they helped keep the village going. My neighbours spoke of the boys at Agios Vassili with a mixture of pity and curiosity. They must be freezing up there, people said. Someone had seen them bathing in the spring – they were skinny like teenagers – and someone else had seen one of them carrying a bag of food up the zigzag path. "Be careful they don't rob you," my neighbours had warned.

I too was curious about the Albanians, but on this afternoon I did not want an interruption to my solitude. I by-passed the cells and climbed straight up to the plain above, where vistas of higher plains and more remote villages opened up; I would visit them another day. I stretched out on the rocky ground and looked out over Arfara and Versova, Evrestina and the sea. My imagination had not lied; the place was as lovely as I had remembered – even more lovely. Why had I wanted to go anywhere else? I fell asleep, or thought I did, the sensation of floating over the village, buoyed by currents of warm air, staying with me. When I opened my eyes I felt deeply refreshed and at peace, as though a blessing had been bestowed.

><

Back at the house, Apostoli had arrived with his truck and a plastic vat of freshly crushed grape juice. An Albanian worker was helping him transfer the juice into a wooden barrel, where it would ferment into wine. Grandfather had always supervised this task, but now that he had passed away, Apostoli had taken it on. Winemaking held little joy for him – often he did not bother making wine for his own use – but he was aware that the local wine meant a great deal to my father, Angelo.

His interest in the wine-maker's art was a legacy from his years in the restaurant. He had learned what he could from drinking, reading and talking wine. But Apostoli, who had laboured over wine grapes all his life, cared little for tastings and for theory; the work of wine-making exhausted him and left little room for pleasure.

This was true of most of the villagers. Only a few families continued to make their own wine. When Apostoli first drove me back to the village, we'd seen a group of Albanians, trousers rolled, jumping on a crimson vat of wine grapes. "Don't Greeks do that any more?" I'd asked. A short, derisory laugh had been his only answer.

The few remaining wine-makers gathered the grapes from vines they left unirrigated, to enhance the flavour and potency of their brew. Their wine-making was basic and straightforward: they crushed the fruit and later added preservative tablets to the barrel. Some would add pine resin too, but my family did not (and who knows why retsina tastes acceptable under a Greek sky but is undrinkable anywhere else?). After a few weeks, the villagers would take the wine to a local chemist, who would advise them whether or not to add sugar to the barrel. As a rule, Grandfather Vassili's wine had not needed additives, although no-one could say why it was superior; the difference was ascribed to good fortune. The wine was a deep gold colour, dry, full-flavoured and deceptively easy to drink. Commercial white wines tasted thin and acidic by comparison.

In the years before the Second World War, wine grapes and

currants had been Chrysambela's main crops. The currants were sold to England to be made into plum puddings and Christmas cakes. The wine was poured into goatskin bags, taken to the coast by mule and donkey, transferred to barrels and then transported by caïque to the arid, wine-starved villages on the opposite side of the gulf. But in the lean years after the war, olives became the dominant crop. Olives provided food as well as cash, and the daily habit of drinking wine went into decline. In recent years, however, the grape had come into its own again; fields that had long lain fallow had been planted with vines. But this wine was made elsewhere and most of the growers took no pride in it; they watered their vines to give the fruit bulk, and picked the grapes green if they had to.

As far as Apostoli was concerned, Angelo's enthusiasm for wine was an unaccountable foreign weirdness, like golf. He stood on the road, cursing freely, while attaching a hose to the plastic vat. "I'm never doing this again," he grumbled. "I've wasted hours and hours on this wretched wine." Angelo stood by, watching and smiling contentedly. Apostoli's bad temper was such an old story that it had become a source of family amusement. As I approached, Apostoli interrupted his invective to ask where I had been and why I had taken so long. "You're not a well person," he called out as I walked up the steps, "you're crazy like your father."

Inside the house, the kitchen was overflowing with welcome gifts: bags of sweet eating grapes from Apostoli, who had remembered my liking for the fruit and insisted they be reserved for me alone; a basket of walnuts from Yiota, along with a dish of *moustoalevra*, a dessert made from the jelly that remained after the wine grapes were crushed; homemade sour dough and a sack of beans from Apostoli's wife, Katina; a basil plant and a bottle of local wine vinegar from kind Vassiliki.

My mother was frying eggplant and Nick, who was married to Apostoli's eldest daughter, Sophia, was talking to her in his characteristic boom. As I poured a glass of wine from the carafe on the table, he turned to me and began outlining his plans for my husband and me to settle in the village and become his partners in a wine-growing enterprise. Nick's dark hair had gone white in my absence, but otherwise he was unchanged: hearty, robust and with a good head for business. He was an officer in the air force and had plans to retire to the village in a few years.

"This place makes you happy," he said, "and it's good for your health. I know you and Tony. You're hard workers and good people, and I'm not someone who pays compliments. I'm serious about this. I could use your help and we would also like the company. What do you say?"

><

THE PLANE TREE

Oasis was the village immediately beyond Chrysambela, about five kilometres away down a winding road. It was a smaller village than ours, and its grip on the future was even more tenuous; only a handful of families remained. Other villages in the region – including our own – were attracting well-to-do Athenians who bought up the abandoned stone dwellings and restored them in a rustic style. But so far, their money and energy had by-passed Oasis. The village was green, prettily situated and had its share of handsome homes; it had once been renowned for the prosperity and diligence of its householders. But it was hidden in a dale. It had no wide views of the sea and the mountains, but looked only at itself.

Oasis's chief glory was the plane tree in its square. Almost every village square in Greece has a plane tree, but the one in Oasis was exceptional, a king of sorts. The tree was very old – although no-one could say exactly how old – and so big that the hollow in its trunk had once served as a chapel. In its prime, the tree's massive limbs had arched over the asphalt square, extending to its outer edges and filling the space with wavering shadows. Eight years had passed since I had last seen it. Then the tree had been sick; the leaves at the tips of the branches were thin and patchy, as though the good sap could no longer extend that far. And because the tree had once been great, even renowned, its sickness affected the atmosphere of the village, so that the houses and the people appeared to take on its melancholy aspect, its green look of decay.

On that visit, I'd met a man whom I had known in Australia, where he had been a drunkard, unable to hold down a job. In an attempt to stem the tide of unhappiness that emigration had unleashed, he had gone back to Greece, men who had emigrated with him contributing the money for his fare. In Oasis he lived as a squatter and earned what he could by gathering wild hyacinth bulbs for the market; returning to the mountains had not renewed his fortunes. He was still wearing shabby clothes when I saw him and his expression was timid and abashed, as though he were continually ashamed. It seemed sadly appropriate that he was living in the shade of the dying tree.

Oasis held a kind of fascination for me. Whenever I heard that someone had visited the village I would ask after the tree. It's still there, they would say. But for how long? Now Paul Connellopoulos, a friend of Angelo's from Melbourne, wanted to visit Oasis. Paul, who was seventy-four, had come to Greece for a family reunion. In particular, he wanted to see his elder brother, Nick, whom he had not seen for forty-two years. Nick was a success: he had emigrated to Venezuela, where he had owned a profitable cheese factory. In Melbourne, Paul had been a real estate agent, but had lacked his brother's aptitude for commerce. His agency had been run in the spirit of the Sufi mystic, who is under instructions to be in the world but not of it. Paul's forebears had been icon painters and his children were artists and musicians.

On this holiday to Greece, his first in more than two decades, Paul was visiting churches around the Peloponnese, accompanied by Nick. They were compiling a photograph album of the icons painted by their father and grandfather; a Descent from the Cross, the work of their father, Sotiri, was believed to be in Oasis, in the church of Agia Marina, and they had arranged to take Angelo and me along with them.

They arrived in Nick's sleek new German car, both looking much younger than their years; Paul, especially, looked almost boyish. Whenever we saw him in Greece, he was dressed as though for a grand occasion; today, he wore a three-piece, grey pinstriped suit, a maroon handkerchief folded in his pocket to match his tie. When Angelo took him onto our balcony to show him the view of Parnassus, Paul's eyes filled with tears. "He hasn't stopped crying since he's been in Greece," said Nick drily.

We piled into the car. Nick drove while Paul and Angelo exclaimed at the scenery. "It's all excellent and wonderful, my friend," said Paul, patting my father on the arm, "all excellent and wonderful."

It was Sunday afternoon and the church was locked. A handsome, straight-backed woman in black, who was tending a vegetable patch nearby, offered to find the priest. "Do not thank me," she said, "this is my duty." She asked who we were and told us her name, Kiria Sotiria. My father recognised it and offered his sympathy on the recent death of her husband; Kiria Sotiria wiped away a tear and grasped his hand in gratitude.

We had interrupted the priest's afternoon sleep. Father Michael Nikoloulopoulos walked over to the church in his long black vestments, wearing the childlike, slightly befuddled expression of the newly woken. He was eighty-nine. His daughter, Tasia, held his arm. "Do not apologise for disturbing him," she said. "We have so few visitors here."

Tasia was also dressed in black; her mother had died the previous year. That death had brought her back to Oasis to look after her father, who had not yet recovered from his loss. "And after so many years together, how can he be expected to recover from such a thing?" she murmured.

Father Michael was a gentle, affable soul. Paul was particularly delighted by him. Whenever the priest spoke, Paul smiled broadly and occasionally interrupted with remarks such as: "How happy I am to talk to you, Father," and "May you live to be a thousand."

Father Michael told us that as a young man he had trained as a barber, working from Oasis's general store, which had also served as a *kafeneion*. In the lean years immediately after the Second World War, a teacher who lived in the nearby village of Vella advised him to enter the priesthood. "I was poor, you see, and he told me that priests always got by." And so he entered the theological school in Corinth.

"I studied Byzantine music," he said proudly. He used to play the mandolin, and before ordination he had been a *psalti* – a lay chanter who accompanies the priest in the singing of the liturgy. After he graduated, Father Michael requested to be transferred to the church at Akrata, the nearest town to Oasis. He wanted to leave the quiet place where had been born. "But they kept me here in the mountains," he said, and shrugged resignedly.

Oasis was small, but Father Michael had his work cut out for him. He farmed whatever land he had, provided for his eight children and performed his church duties. On alternate Sundays he would sing the liturgy at nearby Sinedro, a village with no priest of its own. On Easter Saturday he celebrated the full midnight service in both villages, travelling by donkey in the moonlight to Sinedro once he had finished at Oasis.

Agia Marina was modest and functional, the Descent from the Cross its most ambitious and original painting. The icons in Greek Orthodox churches are generally portraits of the saints, painted in familiar poses. They tend to be stylised and to represent ideals of piety and valour rather than the individuality of the artist or his subject, the spirit rather than flesh and blood. But Sotiri Connellopoulos had trained in Pisa; his Descent was dark and restrained, an exploration of human suffering and dignity in the Italian style. Paul said the work, an oil, had been painted in Egio – a coastal town in the region – and had been exhibited in Paris, where it had won a prize.

How had the painting come to Oasis? Neither the brothers nor Father Michael knew. I realised that if I had come to Agia Marina on a routine visit, the painting would have gone unnoticed; I would not have expected the little church to contain anything out of the ordinary and would have passed over the work, assuming it to be a copy.

Nick took several photographs of the Descent. He was a quiet, undemonstrative man; if seeing his father's painting or meeting

Father Michael had moved him, he did not show it. Paul discovered another icon by his father, a more conventional portrait of St Nicholas on a gold background. He remarked that his father's style was distinctive: the faces were more round-eyed and natural-looking than traditional Byzantine-style faces. I thought I could see a resemblance between Paul's eyes and the eyes of St Nicholas, but that may have been my fancy.

Father Michael said that because of his age, he didn't always perform the Sunday services. Oasis was so small that sometimes a *psalti* could not be found, and it was tiring for him to carry out the service alone. Paul told him that he too had been a *psalti*, when he was a boy in Akrata. Spontaneously, and with an unexpected strength, the two men then began to sing a section of the liturgy together. Their voices, sweet and solemn, rose up and filled the church. Their song silenced us.

Father Michael had accidentally turned on the speaker system, so that the chanting had been heard not only in Agia Marina, but also in the square and all over Oasis.

"Never mind, never mind," said the old man, when he realised what he had done, "it will do the people good." Meanwhile, Paul had turned away, overcome by emotion, his face in his hands.

Before we left Oasis, I asked Father Michael how the plane tree was faring. He told me it had revived after the villagers had ripped up the asphalt in the square. "We were told that it needed to breathe," he said. "So we did what was necessary."

The tree had also been severely pruned. It looked smaller, like a patient who has lost weight after a serious illness. Slender limbs had sprouted from its old branches but they were not yet able to disguise the tree's lopped-off, angular appearance. The operation had robbed the square of the shadowy mystery that I remembered; it was barer, more ordinary now. But there was more light, and with it, the possibility of growth. Though diminished, the tree's vigour had returned against the odds.

>=<

VASSILIKI

I first met Vassiliki during the year Tony and I lived in the village. My first encounter with her was a backward glance, a wave. I saw her early one morning as she was walking back down our front steps, towards the road. By the door were four brown eggs, wrapped in newspaper. Over the previous weeks I had found other gifts there, left by an unknown caller: a bag of freshly picked okra and zucchini; ripe peaches; a dish of wild capers, pickled in vinegar.

Vassiliki was dressed in working clothes, all of them heavy and worn: a headscarf tied under the chin, a man's shirt, a shapeless drill skirt, plastic shoes and men's socks.

"Thank you," I called out.

"It's nothing." And she raised her hand in a wave.

Vassiliki wouldn't come in for coffee, as the cool hours immediately after the dawn were the best time for work, but she promised to do so another day. And she did return, more than once, to sit and talk, although she never stayed for long. Usually she came by in the early evening, perhaps with a dish of salty, freshly roasted pumpkin seeds.

Vassiliki lived in a small, low-ceilinged, makeshift house where the only comforts were the tubs of basil and wild cyclamen that lined the courtyard. She washed by hand and cooked on a gas jet or a wood-fired stove; her kitchen was a lean-to facing the yard. But she and her husband had supervised, and largely financed, the building of their son's holiday house next door, an elegant, double-storeyed place with parquet floors, an all-electric kitchen and a bathroom of dazzling whiteness. Her son had offered his parents the use of the bathroom while he and his family were away, but Vassiliki confessed that all those gleaming tiles intimidated her. She preferred to leave their upkeep to her daughter-in-law and to stick to the simple things she knew.

Vassiliki recalled the past as a series of poetic vignettes, although whether the poetry of an episode led her to remember it, or whether she had made poetry from the memories that were left her, it was impossible to say. For the elderly, the most vivid memories reside in the place to which their imagination has retreated. But the past signified more than youth to most of these villagers; it was also a time of extraordinary suffering. The German occupation and the Greek civil war still cast their shadow over the collective memory of Chrysambela.

When the Germans arrived in 1941, Vassiliki was only sixteen. She still remembered the heavy *tak, tak, tak* of German boots as they marched outside the door. In those days, the road to Versova was a muddy mule track; the Germans could only make it there on foot. This gave the villagers, who had wide views over the valleys and an intimate knowledge of the country-side, an advantage. They posted a twenty-four-hour watch at strategic points, such as the Saracen's Mount or the church of the Prophet Elijah, and sounded the alarm when the Germans were in sight. Their families would then take to the fields, often camping for days in the mud-brick summer houses hidden among the currant vines until the danger was over.

Vassiliki told me of a day when she left the relative safety of her family's summer house to walk back to the village; she wanted to check on her sister, Panagiota, who had been too sick to leave their house. On her way, Vassiliki passed a threshing ground, an elevated place that also served as a lookout. German soldiers were there, standing over a man from Versova who was suspected of being part of the Resistance. She hid and watched as they shot him and left his body on the ground.

When she reached the village, she found that her sister was no better. The family were fatalistic about her sickness; they'd recognised tuberculosis, and called upon the Almighty to do what He could. In those years they had barely enough to eat and little money to spare for doctors and such. While Vassiliki was nursing Panagiota, they were discovered by an Italian soldier. They were frightened, but the soldier did not loot the house – it was practically bare – nor did he threaten the girls; the Italians were not cruel. When the soldier saw Vassiliki's sister, he cried out in pity and grabbed Vassiliki's arm. "Medicine, medicine," he said in his broken Greek, "she needs medicine." Her sister was so wretched, and the Italian so emphatic, that Vassiliki decided to follow his advice. She resolved to walk to Derveni, a seaside town about twenty kilometres away, to buy what she could from the chemist. Her father agreed to the scheme, and gave her the little money he had. But the Italian's warning came too late, and soon after, her sister died.

When Vassiliki talked about her life, the Second World War was a painful – but incidental – event; she was still a child, still living in her father's house. Her greatest trials, she believed, came with marriage. Then the poverty of the household was hers to manage, the hard work fell on her hands, and during the most difficult years – the first two decades of her married life – she lived in subservience to her mother-in-law, or *pethera*.

It was the custom for a young wife to move into her husband's childhood home. Brides would enter a house with a dowry – woven blankets, embroidered sheets, a parcel of land – only to find that despite their most prized possessions, their gifts of youth and love, they were placed at the bottom of the household hierarchy. Brides were expected to submit not only to their husband's authority, but also to the rule of his parents. Mothers-in-law, who in all likelihood had endured years of petty tyranny themselves, were often determined to exercise whatever power they had. It was once common to set difficult tasks for young brides as a test of their worth. Loading up a mule with a thorny plant used for kindling was an old favourite. Each stage of the process was fraught: stooping to cut branches from the small, prickly bush; tying them together, when it was impossible not to cut your hands; loading the animal without causing it to bolt; leading it back to the house and then unloading and stacking the twigs.

Even if the *pethera* was kindly, problems arose because of the rigid etiquette of duty and respect that all good girls observed. My Grandmother Katerina, for example, had no cruelty in her, but she was superstitious. She insisted that Katina, her *nifi*, or daughter-in-law, stay in her room for forty days following the birth of each of her three children, so as to ward off the evil eye. Even after four decades, my aunt was unable to recall those forced seclusions without bitterness.

Vassiliki was proud that she had paid her dues to her *pethera* without taking her revenge. When the old woman was on her deathbed, Vassiliki laid aside her household duties to nurse her as best she could. "At the end she could no longer speak, but by the way she held on to my hand, and looked into my eyes, I knew that I had done the right thing by her and that she was grateful to me."

She told me that story during the olive season, because of a scandal which was then unfolding. Old Chryssoula was dying. For more than thirty years she had lived with her son and his wife in a family in which the men were passive and the women were strong. The *nifi* and Chryssoula had struggled relentlessly for power in the house, their malice unrestrained by shame or the threat of approbation. Chryssoula condemned her *nifi* as a slattern, while the *nifi* warned Chryssoula that she would pay a heavy price for her sharp tongue one day. And now, with the onset of winter, the old lady's time had come. She had a fever and was so weak that she could not leave her bed without assistance, yet her family still left at dawn to work in the fields, leaving her home alone all the long day. Those few villagers who were not picking olives – old ladies themselves for the most part – would hear her crying out for help or company. They would warm her lunch and feed her, change her linen if it was soiled, and heat the room.

The once fierce old lady would bestow her blessings upon them. "May you always be refreshed," she said to Vassiliki one day as she sat beside her, peeling mandarins, "as your gift refreshes me now."

"She's as cold as a bone in there," Vassiliki told me. "The air is so cold you can see your breath, and her sheets are icy."

Occasionally someone would challenge the *nifi*: "What if the old lady dies while you're away?"

"So what?" would come the reply. "She'll still be there when we get back."

Vassiliki knew that Chryssoula's son bore some responsibility for the state his mother was in, but like most of the villagers, she blamed the *nifi*. According to her code, the family's moral standing was in the woman's hands.

Vassiliki was now a *pethera* herself. Far from being feared, however, she worked to please her son's well-educated, Athenian wife. Most sons no longer farmed the land; few remained with their parents. A *nifi* who was prepared to regularly visit the village was praised. She was no longer set trials of the old kind because, Lord knows, these trips to the country, with its mud and tedium, were trial enough. Gathering crops, planting vegetables, feeding the animals – the common round of village work – were considered beneath the young women. I often wondered how such a huge shift in perception had come about in a single generation; in part it was a reaction against the drudgery and poverty of narrow village ways, but I was never able to explain it completely.

Vassiliki regretted her loneliness and she hated the stench of Athens, but she had nevertheless urged her sons to find jobs in the city: there lay security, prestige and ease of living. Her faith in education, in cash, in progress, came down to this: she did not want her own sufferings to be repeated. And so she did not resent her daughter-in-law's abhorrence of village life. It was natural for young people to want more, she said, that was what their parents had worked for. But I was never impressed by the Athenian disdain for village life; it was an affectation that would have been comic if it were not the most important single reason why the villages were dying. The advent of the European Community and its guaranteed markets meant that a comfortable income could be made from the olives and grapevines around Chrysambela, but despite this most young people continued to leave. They preferred not to soil their hands.

Vassiliki was kind to me partly because of the year I had spent living in the village, in defiance of the strictures of fashion and taste. But mostly she was kind because it was her nature. She seldom spoke ill of her neighbours, a rare quality in a small community, and was known for the generosity with which she treated her Albanian workers. But I believe that her kindness to me was also motivated, at least in part, by her loyalty to a particular memory from her childhood, which I reminded her of by virtue of my blood. And it was a story that she liked to tell: the unforgettable afternoon that she spent with my father's elder brother, Nicko.

This was in the years before the war, when she and Nicko were in primary school. They were walking through the fields together, by the stream at the bottom of the valley, when they saw two *nereids*, or water nymphs, combing their long hair and singing as they sat near the water. Vassiliki said the nymphs were big, and beautiful she supposed, but frightening too. Nicko was a bold, handsome, capable boy, but the sight of the nymphs was too much for him. His face turned white, his hands shook, and he ran away, calling on the Virgin to protect him. So intense was his fear that it overpowered Vassiliki's milder feelings of quiet astonishment. *Nereids* were held by some to be a sign of ill omen. It might be that what Nicko feared was not the water nymphs themselves, but the warning they brought him of what was to come.

Nicko was the second oldest boy in a family of five sons, and so able and hard-working that people talked as though he was the one who would take over Grandfather Vassili's fields. But when he was twelve, he fell from his horse near a bridge that crossed the stream where he had seen the water nymphs.

Grandmother Katerina never recovered from the shock of seeing her son's corpse carried into the yard, all bloodied and trampled. The grief that rose up stayed with her for the rest of her days. On the rare occasions when it lifted, my father said that the house would be filled with her happiness and the surprise of it. But just as abruptly the shutter would close again, and joy was suspended, out of reach. Her mother, Great-grandmother Sophia, said a dark spell had been put on Katerina, and blamed the evil eye. But the events of Katerina's life were explanation enough. She lost another son to cot death, lived through the German occupation and the civil war, and then saw two sons emigrate to Australia. Her mother took her on pilgrimages, and together they prayed for Katerina's melancholy to be cured. It never was.

I asked Vassiliki if anyone saw *nereids* around Chrysambela these days. No, she said, not any more. People's heads were so full now, you see, everyone was so clever and educated, that the world looked different; maybe it *was* different. But when she was a girl, she had known very little. She tapped her skull with a knuckle: there had been ample room in there for the nymphs and their strange song.

Grandfather Vassili had also believed in water nymphs, although he was a tough, hard-working man who did not allow his superstitions to disable him. After his wife died, the *nereids* often kept him awake at night, calling out for him and banging on his window. His response had been characteristically pragmatic: he had refused to join them and had locked the window tight.

><

WALKS WITH ANGELO

My father has a good memory. Even though he has not lived in Versova for fifty years, he remembers stories that the villagers themselves have forgotten; stories that have been laid aside, overtaken by the accumulated weight of everyday events, live on in him.

"See that woman," he once said to my cousin Peter and me, pointing through our living room windows to Dimitra, a sweet-faced crone who was leading her loaded donkey down the road. "Well, her father committed the worst crime to take place here. He was cuckolded, you see, but instead of facing up to his wife and the man concerned, he threatened the man's son, an innocent schoolboy, with a gun. He fired shots into the ground – just out of stupidity, to frighten the boy. So the boy ran away of course, but one of the shots ricocheted off a stone and killed him."

"What happened to Dimitra's father?" I asked.

"He was jailed. She spent her childhood in poverty because her mother could barely earn enough to feed them."

Peter liked to listen to my father talk and would encourage him, in his quiet way, with artfully placed questions. "Are you sure that was the worst crime?" And together they would weigh up other contenders. The young girl who, more than thirty years ago, stabbed old man Gregory to death in the *kafeneion* was the most notorious case, but hard to evaluate because the girl's motives were still not known. By unspoken consent, the crimes that were committed during the civil war were placed in a separate category and were not included in the discussion.

But the stories I was most interested in, the ones that built up the picture of Angelo's childhood, were not spoken of so casually. Scraps, hints and partial glimpses were all I ever got from him. In part, this was because he and I were unpractised at talking and listening to each other. While I was growing up, Angelo had spent most of his time working in his restaurant. Those lost years remained a barrier between us; a continuous cold front. Unstable emotions threatened to overtake even our simplest exchanges, and we had discovered that avoiding conversation was less hurtful than subjecting ourselves to these inchoate and unpredictable gusts of feeling. So much time had been lost that we were no longer comfortable with each other, and this lack of ease was painful for us both. I had hoped that once we were in Greece, the power of the physical setting would help melt away these obstacles, but so far this had not been the case.

One day, Vassiliki told me a story she'd heard from her Albanian workers about a Greek man from a village near Corinth. He had employed an illegal immigrant for a season, paid him nothing, then, when the Albanian complained, silenced him by hitting him over the head with a spade and throwing his corpse into a ravine. I had no idea whether the story was true (although Vassiliki believed it) but thought it an interesting antidote to the endless Greek scaremongering about the Albanians; it showed how frightened and suspicious and, above all, how vulnerable the Albanians were. But when I told this story to my father, our conversation quickly veered out of control. In no time we were rowing, with unnecessary heat, about gullibility, trust and the nature of truth.

Discouraged and exhausted, I sat on the balcony to clear my head and wished for Mt Parnassus to appear. Our house was next door to the village primary school. A handful of students were shouting and laughing as they ran through the small pine forest that shaded the schoolyard. Angelo had helped plant those trees as a boy. They reminded me of one of the few stories I'd heard about his early years. When he was ten he went to the high school in Akrata, the same school where my cousin Peter now taught mathematics. Today, the few teenagers left in the village travel to Akrata by bus, but in my father's day there was no bus – because there was no road. Once a week, he and his older brother

Dino walked the fifteen kilometres down the mountain and over a valley to Akrata, where they shared a room; on the weekend the boys walked back to the village (or, in my father's words, he ran back, so happy was he to be going home). Once a week, Grandfather Vassili would bring them supplies on his donkey: bread, olive oil, dried beans, firewood for cooking. Akrata was full of schoolchildren, mostly boys, who lived in this way. During the years of the German occupation, a strict curfew was enforced and the boys stayed indoors after dark, studying in unheated rooms.

When I was a child, Angelo's account of his school days made a great impression on me; so bleak and austere, like the sad part of a fairy tale. It was a story that deserved a happy ending, but instead his early exile from the village was followed by the greater exile of emigration. In the tradition of Greek migrants, Angelo doggedly pursued financial success in businesses of his own. But prosperity when it came was clouded by the regret that it had been so hard won. Each gain was shot through with ambivalence.

I looked out over the valley and thought how a map of my father's past could be read in the folds of the land, with the distant Gulf of Corinth representing the world beyond Chrysambela, the foreign place where he had spent most of his life. The next day I persuaded Angelo to set off down the mountain with me to retrace part of the journey he had made as a schoolboy, when he had walked with his brother on a muddy mule track, all the way to Akrata.

><

There is much to be said for talking as you walk. What you say is not the sole focus, so the pressure to perform – to impress – is off. If the conversation lags or is strained, the silence falls naturally enough; the compensations of landscape and exercise fill the vacuum. Listening can also be easier on the hoof. Expressions of pain or amusement remain private: no-one is looking at you. And if a story sends you spinning into a reverie so that, on emerging from the eddy of your thoughts, you find you have nothing to say, well, then it doesn't matter. The walking takes over.

On our first walk our path followed an asphalt road, and people would occasionally stop to offer us a lift, clucking their tongues in astonishment when we told them that we preferred to go on foot. The notion of walking for its own sake was a novelty in the village and was regarded, at best, with an amused indulgence.

One morning, years before, Apostoli had driven me along the same road that I was now taking with my father. Rain clouds parted over the crest of Evrestina, and I exclaimed at the beauty of it.

"These mountains, these mountains!" Apostoli shouted at me in response. "How weary I am of them – don't mention them to me. I wish they would go crashing into the sea."

His outburst was so violent and unexpected that it was funny. I turned my face away, but too late.

"What's happened to you?" he asked. "Are you laughing?"

I nodded helplessly.

"That's because you don't understand what it means to be trapped here for a lifetime," he said, but the edge of his anger had gone. He was bad-tempered but soft-hearted; it pleased him when his outbursts did not give offence.

Angelo had not lived in the mountains long enough to grow disenchanted with them. From the time he left the village to go to school, the high country represented refuge and escape. When he arrived in Akrata as a schoolboy in 1941, the Germans were a hostile presence. Any gains made by the Greek Resistance meant the arbitrary slaughter of civilians, thirty Greeks being executed for every German soldier killed. Angelo recalled seeing bodies strung up on poles along the road into the town. Once, at the railway station, he saw a German soldier kick a boy off a train, sending him sprawling onto the platform, his tray of dried fruit upended. The boy was about his own age; he had been punished for having the temerity to enter the carriage first.

Our first walk took us to a mud-brick *kafeneion* that had long fallen into disrepair. From here, a track veered into a scrubby, eroded valley that led to Akrata. Angelo pointed out the village of Ambelos in the distance. When he was a child, the village was called Velkouvina and was occupied only in winter, when its inhabitants came down from Rahova in the high country, bringing their animals and their bedding with them. They planted crops that flourished in the sun, mostly olives and citrus fruit, but their holdings were small; this was merely subsistence farming. Velkouvina had no running water, only a single well, and its houses were mean and shabby; in the summer, the villagers returned to the slopes of Rahova to plant vegetable gardens and to tend their sheep. Rahova was then a substantial community with a post office and a theological college. But now the fortunes of the villages had been reversed: Ambelos was a prosperous suburb of Akrata, while Rahova, like its neighbour Vella, teetered on the edge of extinction.

Only a generation ago, people had spent their lives moving up and down the mountains according to the seasons. Versova, where Angelo was born, was the exception. It was not high enough, or cold enough, to warrant an annual migration. Angelo's loyal conviction that his village was the ideal place – the Camelot of Achaïa – was once shared by Turkish pashas. They lived there, ruled from there, and even built a mosque in the square, with a minaret so broad that a horse could be ridden to the top. It was demolished after the Peloponnese was liberated in 1822 and the village church of Agios Apostoli was built on its foundations.

Angelo enjoyed talking about the history of the village, and our conversation meandered pleasantly as we followed the road back to Versova. We took a short cut, stopping at an old threshing ground with wide views of the valley and the gulf. Angelo had long dreamed of building a house on the site but Grandfather Vassili, who once owned the land, had given it to a poor neighbour years before; the plot was small and unproductive and so had had little value in Vassili's eyes. Although Angelo now owned an equally well sited house of his own, he was unable to pass the spot without a sigh of regret.

As we stood there, old Maria emerged from her nearby house and asked us what we had been up to. She was a tiny woman, dressed in black, with a shrill voice and a high, tinny laugh. Behind her glasses, her eyes wrinkled with pleasure at our chance meeting. In her sombre clothes, she was as merry and bright-eyed as a sprightly black bird.

"Ah, you've been reminiscing about the bad old days I see," she said. "When we were always covered in mud and had to cut wood for the fire just to make a cup of coffee." And she let out her piercing laugh. "But then you went to Australia and escaped all that, my boy," she continued, patting Angelo's arm. "But only just, only just. It was a near thing."

205

What did she mean? Old Maria savoured my bewilderment for a moment and then warmed to her story. "Well," she said, "of course you know that in the bad days of the civil war, Grandfather Vassili's life was in danger. He had helped a soldier from the Government side escort some prisoners down the mountain, and ever after, the *andartes* wanted to kill him."

I had known nothing of the sort. All I knew was that Vassili was sympathetic to the Right, even though his children were all Leftists; when he was alive, heated political arguments had been a household staple.

One night, continued Maria, Grandfather Vassili had climbed through her bedroom window, wearing only his long johns; the *andartes* were coming and he needed a hiding place. He spent the night standing in the fireplace while Maria and her husband, Spiro, lay sleepless in their bed, terrified for their own lives. They knew that if the *andartes* found Vassili, they would also pay dearly.

Although no harm came to Vassili that night, it was eventually decided to evacuate the family to Egira on the coast, where the army lodged them in a safe house. On the day they left, Great-grandmother Sophia gave Maria a bag of gold coins and asked her to bring it down to the coast when the road was safe. The money would be used to pay Angelo's air fare to Australia: he was in his final year of high school and almost seventeen, at which age he would be eligible for the draft.

The responsibility of delivering the bag of coins weighed heavily on Maria. Sophia feared being hijacked by *andartes* on the road to the coast, a legitimate fear that Maria shared. But who was to say that the *andartes* would not steal the money from her? And if they did, there was the added concern that the Kiziloses might not believe it, that they would make enemies of their neighbours, and that she and Spiro, God forbid, might even be held responsible for Angelo's life.

Maria knew that someone in the village had already prevented one of the family from escaping to Australia. The year before, Dino had been ready to benefit from Sophia's golden bag, but he had already turned seventeen and it was illegal for someone of draftable age to emigrate. Vassili used his influence in the village to change Dino's papers to make it appear that he had been born a year later. Vassili had no qualms about doing this, and years later his family had no shame about confessing to it; despite the differences in their political sympathies, they all regarded the civil war as an evil to be avoided by whatever means possible.

Dino packed his bags, said his goodbyes and travelled to Athens to pick up his passport before boarding the plane. But a villager with a grievance against his family informed the passport office that his papers were false; Dino was arrested and detained overnight. The civil war was full of such stories: it was a time when petty grudges blossomed darkly into vengeful acts which had the power to determine a neighbour's fate.

Maria sighed at these memories and tightened her grip on Angelo's arm. He was wearing his usual expression of smiling geniality. I knew from experience that he sometimes wore his smile as a mask – he was unusually inscrutable for a Greek – but it reassured old Maria. She continued her story.

As soon as practicable, she and Spiro had walked down to Egira, taking the bag of money with them. But as they rounded a bend they saw that on the lower reaches of the track the *andartes* had set up a checkpoint and were searching everyone who passed, in order to appropriate money and food. They were not sure what to do: if they turned back they would arouse suspicion, but going on was fraught with risk. And so Spiro discreetly threw the bag of money into the fields, aiming at the base of two cypresses; the trees would serve as a landmark. The bag lay exposed on the grass; all the couple could do was pray that no-one discovered the loot before they returned.

As it happened, luck was on their side: two days later, they found the money untouched. And a month after that Angelo was on a flight to Australia.

Maria smiled up at him with a mixture of triumph and tenderness. Angelo thanked her for the story, and said we had to get back to the house; he suddenly looked very tired.

As we walked on, I considered the chain of seemingly random chances to which my father's fate had been subjected. If Dino had been allowed to board the plane with his false papers, would there have been enough gold coins left for Angelo to emigrate too? And what would have become of him if someone had discovered the bag of coins on the ground? The war ended a few months after he arrived in Sydney. If Angelo had stayed in Greece, in all likelihood he would have passed his high school examinations, and been accepted into university and a life I couldn't imagine. He would not have met my mother and I would not have been born.

I asked him if he had known the story of the gold coins.

"No," he said. "No, I never heard it before."

Yet he had expressed no surprise during Maria's narration. On the way home he said very little.

><

That evening I visited Apostoli and Katina. The story of the gold coins had whetted my curiosity and I wanted to ask Apostoli about his time with the Resistance.

Apostoli only spoke tenderly about the mountains when describing the excellence of the local olive oil, or when talking about his time as a partisan. A stomach operation he'd undergone as a teenager had made him ineligible for the army, but he'd become briefly involved in the Resistance towards the end of the German occupation. While he was with the partisans he'd walked to places in the mountains where he'd never been before or since. Perhaps the strain of making these treks during a time of great danger caused him to perceive the landscape differently, for I once heard him speak, with a trace of awe in his voice, about the unforgiving wildness of the high country, with its wolves and deep snow.

Those years also left him with a taste for cowboy movies. He would often stay up after midnight to watch them, despite the uncertain reception and barely legible subtitles flickering across his television screen. The gunfights, the brawls, the hardship, the uncomplaining manliness, the rough justice – all of it reminded him of the adventure of being an *andarte*.

But when I asked him about what he done and seen during that terrible time, he scowled dismissively and said he didn't want to talk about it. "Bah! Compared to other people, I did nothing. I know nothing. I forbid you to write a word about me."

"Why don't you help the girl?" interrupted Katina. "Is it so hard to tell her what you know? I would talk to you myself, my dear, but I can barely remember a thing. I'm completely useless to you." She smiled at me encouragingly, before glaring at her husband.

But Apostoli was staring into the open fire with a preoccupied expression, and he didn't notice Katina. "Christos Menzelopoulos is the one you should talk to," he said eventually. "He has a greater story to tell than anyone else around these parts. He really was a hero. He saved a lot of people's lives, and he went through a lot himself. It might be tricky, though; he likes to keep to himself."

I knew that although Christos had been born in Versova, he no longer lived there; but his half-brother, Pano, still did. Vassiliki had already told me part of the family's story. At the beginning of the war, when the German occupation had just begun, joining the Resistance had a romantic appeal. Vassiliki remembered Christos Menzelopoulos recruiting for the guerrilla army; he gave her a hat and she went home thrilled, determined to run away to the mountains. Later that evening, Christos's half-brother Apostoli dropped by with some Communist Party newspapers for her father.

"Are you a guerrilla too?" she asked him.

Her interest alarmed her father, who warned her sharply not to talk about what she did not understand. It was winter, and she spent the cold evening sitting on her balcony and listening as Apostoli Menzelopoulos sat under the plane tree in the square, singing songs about freedom, fighting and the caress of a gun.

"Why are you listening to him?" asked her father.

"Because he sings so well."

Vassiliki never saw Apostoli Menzelopoulos again. He became an officer in the Resistance and perished in the dying days of the civil war. His body was never found; in all likelihood, he died in the mountains beyond Chrysambela during the infamous winter of 1948 and '49, when the remnants of the guerrilla army on the Peloponnese fled to the high country, where they were defeated by starvation and exposure. The previous year, his sister, Angeliki, was also recruited by the Left – much against her will, because it was clear by then that the partisans were fighting a lost cause; she was killed by a bomb dropped by a

Government plane as she hid in a summer house in the fields above Arfara.

Meanwhile, their oldest brother, Pano, was conscripted and served with the Government troops for a year. Because he came from a family of active Leftists, the army did not trust him with a gun and he was assigned to shoemaking duty in the Agrapha mountains of northern Greece. On his release from the army, Pano was punished for his political sympathies and did time on the island of Makronissos, where he served a brief sentence of hard labour but escaped the beatings and torture meted out to those who were considered more committed Communists. When he eventually returned to the village, he learned that Apostoli and Angeliki had died; as for Christos, his half-brother, he was in jail, awaiting execution for murder.

And Pano had more trials to overcome. During his conscription and imprisonment, his neighbours had ransacked his house; perhaps they had assumed that he was ill-fated like his siblings and would not return. Pano somehow had to find the courage to live among people who had stolen his property and who had fought his family as enemies. Fifty years later he could not tell the story without weeping. "How did I feel? Like a leaf that is blown by the wind, here and there, with no power of its own at all."

≥◄

Our house was the last one in the old village of Versova. Arfara began on the other side of the road, where a local builder and his brother had constructed two elaborate cement houses for themselves and their families. The size and expense of these houses, with their attics and multiple chimneys, alarmed me, but they were not unique: all of Arfara was gradually being transformed by a mini building boom.

Athenians – often descendants of the villagers – were restoring the old stone houses with care and taste, rebuilding the wooden balconies and fixing traditional brass fittings to the doors. Outsiders were also coming in, buying up land and building follies of their own. They in turn had infected the residents, who, perhaps for the first time in their lives, were spending money on aesthetics, replacing the terracotta tiles on their roofs or opening up old fireplaces. The activity gave Arfara an air of vitality, but also one of unpredictability. Wealth was opening up new vistas of arbitrariness; necessity no longer ruled the mountains.

At the far end of Arfara, for instance, a Greek millionaire was said to be planning a private zoo in the grounds of his grand new home; from my balcony I could hear his workers tirelessly levelling roads and putting up fences. And there was Roy, the retired British theatre director (he was rumoured to have once been married to a famous film star) who lived in a whitewashed cottage with two dogs and the occasional Albanian boarder; almost every afternoon he would walk his dogs past our house, wearing a pained 'don't disturb me' expression. Then there was the stonemason from Epiros who had painstakingly constructed a house in the style of his region, with arches and a courtyard. Epirot stonemasons are renowned throughout Greece, but in Arfara, such a house was a handsome incongruity.

The stonemason's house echoed the ruined dwellings in Vella, a village further up the mountain, whose charm lay both in the remote austerity of its setting and in the integrity of its ruins: crumbling stone piles with stables on the ground floor and great wooden beams in the ceilings. Vella had been founded, centuries before, by Epirots who had walked there – just as the illegal immigrants still did – from their homeland near the Albanian border. But in all likelihood the stonemason's gesture of continuity with Vella was unintended. The various threads of village life were no longer intertwined; the patterns that they made were accidental.

Outsiders have always passed through these mountains. In Angelo's childhood, the strangers were mostly peddlers or traders, whose visits were as regulated as the seasons: the blind man who hawked sultanas and roasted chickpeas at the Feast of Agios Apostoli; the fisherman from Corinth who sold fresh sardines from his van; the man who exchanged old olive oil for soap; gypsies selling rugs and telling fortunes; coopers who would caulk the barrels before the grape harvest; copper merchants selling and repairing pots and pans; *kareklades* – chair men – who repaired the fraying weave on rush-bottomed chairs; travelling musicians who played at the local festivals.

And then came the visitors from the chattering diaspora, the Greeks from the States, Australia, Canada, Germany and Africa who returned to the country every summer in a flurry of boastful affluence and sentimental melancholia. I remember when the man who was said to be the richest Greek in Sydney visited the village. His sister and her husband were the village drunks; they lived in a tumbledown house with an unsteady balcony and did odd jobs in exchange for money and wine. The rich man stayed with them, stocked their pantry with good food, went for walks and reminisced. In the mornings he could be seen on their ramshackle balcony, drinking coffee in his burgundy silk dressing gown, looking for all the world as though he were on his verandah overlooking Sydney Harbour.

The villagers had mixed feelings – partly compassionate, partly envious – about the migrants who came back. The returnees were rarely asked about their foreign lives. At first I interpreted this as indifference, but later came to see it as a type of helplessness: the village was so small and the world was so vast, how could questions alone bridge the gap between them?

As a child, my father heard adults tell strange tales about the *castingari*. All he knew about this creature was that it lived in America, where anyone wishing to immigrate had to confront it. The *castingari* was feared because it was capricious; not everybody was able to get past the beast. Angelo recalled one would-be immigrant, a simpleton, who sailed all the way to New York and then all the way back to the village again, where he climbed a wild pear tree and sat in it until his neighbours found him.

"What are you doing up there?" they asked him. "Why aren't you in America?"

"I couldn't go in because of the *castingari*."

It took Angelo many years to realise that the *castingari* was the customs gate on New York's Ellis Island.

Some years after the First World War, Angelo's grandfather made the long trip to Ellis Island with his thirteen-year-old son. The old man arrived in Manhattan still wearing his traditional pleated white skirt, or *foustanela*. The story goes that when he landed, he looked at the burgeoning city around him and spat on the ground; he returned to Greece after only twelve months. Back in the village he cut an unusual figure, as he was one of the few returned migrants who did not regret leaving the New World behind him. His son remained alone in Manhattan and worked as a shoeshine boy. By the time he was twenty, he owned two restaurants; he then put himself through night school and became a civil engineer. The money he earned helped support the family in the lean years before and after the German occupation. His photo in an oval frame still hangs in the house where he was born. Yet he was hardly known by the people who still honour him, as he died many years ago, alone in America.

That photo, with its promise of renewal, was one more reason why Angelo had left for Australia. But now the long cycle of leaving had ended, and the village was slowly filling up again. For the most part, the outsiders were welcomed. They had little interest in tilling the soil, but no matter, their grand buildings were something to talk about; and, more importantly, they connected the village with the wider world. Living in a museum of old Greek values had only a limited appeal for the people who were stuck in it.

>×<

Directly above the chapel of Agios Dimitri in Arfara was a plain so high that it looked onto the flat crest of Evrestina. On this lonely and elevated spot, an Athenian accountancy firm had plans to build a holiday village for its staff. It had already purchased the land and signs pointing to the 'Ikismos Logiston' – the Accountants' Settlement – had been erected on the road that led up from Egira.

One morning at the end of November, just after the first snows of the winter had fallen, I decided to take a walk up to the high plain. Angelo was reluctant to come with me: it was too far and he couldn't see the point of it. He looked upwards, casting a baleful eye at the snow. The higher you walked, the deeper it was, and the more treacherous the roads.

215

"Don't come then, I'll go by myself. I don't mind, it's not that far."

It was a sunny, still day. The snow had made the mountains unfamiliar: Evrestina's umber face had turned white, as had all of Arfara. Every horizontal surface was clean and iced; even the bare, upturned arms of the cherry trees supported a delicate line of whiteness.

Angelo watched as I headed off, then grabbed his coat and joined me. It would be a hard walk, but although my father was sixty-four, he was fitter than I was; a climb that would leave me gasping would see him standing at the crest of the hill, unpuffed and censorious.

The climb into Arfara is steep. We laboured up a zigzagging road and were soon high above our house; looking down, we heard a child's laughter rising effortlessly through the air, as though in greeting.

As we approached the square in Arfara, we saw a group of village women wearing trousers under their skirts and scarves tied under their chins, nodding and talking about the snow. It was an unusually heavy fall for this time of year; if the weather turned any colder it would affect the olive harvest. There was general concern about the growing unpredictability of the seasons, but the conversation ended when someone said, "*Ti na kanoume?*" – What can we do? – the standard Greek response to all matters outside personal control. Then everybody smiled and the women waved us on; on such a morning it was impossible to be downcast for too long.

It was a weekday and some of the finest, most substantial houses we passed were boarded up because their owners lived elsewhere. Angelo soon forgot that he had been unwilling to come with me, and began talking about the occupants of houses that he recognised and the stories that he knew about them. We passed the austere, double-storey house where Kostandinos, the pharmacist, had lived. He had been a gentle man and an idealist, said Angelo. After the German occupation ended, Kostandinos made plans to join the guerrillas. Grandfather Vassili, although a right-winger, recognised the goodness in the man and urged him not to throw away his life; everybody knew the *andartes* were fighting a lost cause. But, explained Angelo, that was exactly why Kostandinos went. He was stationed in the mountains just above Arfara and somehow survived the last, devastating winter of the war. Occasionally he would be sighted by the villagers; although he was armed, nobody feared him. Stories were told about how thin and weak he was, barely more than a skeleton.

After the civil war had officially ended, a bounty was put on the pharmacist's head. One day, one of his fellow villagers, a farmer, spotted him while he was out hunting. Remembering the bounty, he shot Kostandinos.

About forty years later, the farmer who killed Kostandinos died after catching his leg in a tractor, the driver dragging the body along behind him for some time before realising what had happened. When the dead man's neighbours – people who had lived with him on good enough terms for decades – heard about the accident, they quietly agreed that the farmer had deserved his gruesome death: justice had at last been done.

I asked Angelo about another house, one of the few big buildings in the village that remained untouched. He said it had once been the home of the four Philopoulos boys, all of whom had been executed by the *andartes* during the Occupation. I had admired the house just moments before, but now it took on a sombre cast and I noticed how neglected it looked, as though still in mourning.

In the higher reaches of Arfara, the snow was deep and untrodden. On such a day, the sadness of my father's stories did not infect me for long. The views, the exercise and the brilliant air made me as heedless and as happy as a drunk. *Ti na kanoume?* The phrase came unbidden.

The road ahead had been churned up by the frozen footsteps of mountain sheep – since the snow had fallen, a shepherd and his flock had been the only others to have walked this far. We followed their tracks up the steep bend that led to the chapel of Agios Dimitri and the Accountants' Settlement on the plain above.

We were both pleased to have climbed so high, but I was badly out of breath. I swallowed great gulps of air as Angelo looked on disapprovingly. When I recovered, we pushed open the chapel door and went inside. It was a neglected, dusty place; all the oil in the lamps had dried and faded spring flowers were still garlanded around the icon of St Dimitri. The style of the icons was familiar; we realised they had been painted by Sotiri Connellopoulos. I took photographs of St Dimitri, a Madonna and Child and a John the Baptist for Paul's album, certain that the remote chapel would not have made it onto his list of pilgrimage sites.

Next to the chapel grew a big, gnarled holly tree. During the summer sunsets the tree was visible from Versova, silhouetted against the sky. In the days when everyone in the district had travelled on foot, the chapel and the tree had been important landmarks. I remembered a story that Vassiliki had told me about the place. When she was a girl, her father had travelled by mule to a village far away, on the other side of the mountains, where he had some business to take care of. It was winter, bitterly cold, and on his way home, as night fell, it began to snow. There were no roads, just a track, and her father began to fear that he would lose his way. But then he saw a light in the distance and realised it must be Agios Dimitri. The sight steadied him. Once he reached the chapel, he knew he would be on familiar territory and that it would be a relatively simple matter to make his way downhill to the village below. From their house there, Vassiliki's mother also saw the distant light through the falling snow. She was superstitious, in the manner of village women, and was worried about her husband, who was late; the light heartened her and she said a prayer. When her husband finally came home, chilled and exhausted, he said he believed the light had saved his life. Together the whole family gave thanks, not only to the unknown person who had lit the lamp, but also to the saint who had inspired them to do so.

Our last stop was the high plain where the accountants planned to build their holiday homes. A solitary wild pear tree grew there, and beyond it more mountains rose. What would happen to that thorny tree, I wondered, when the accountants moved in? Resentment towards these strangers welled up in me. Would they care about the stories with which this land was laden? The stories that Angelo and the villagers told? These stories bound the villagers to the place so intimately, so dearly, that even the stones, it seemed, carried a secret history. I muttered something about accountants not understanding the mystery of the plain and Angelo laughed at me. There was nothing intrinsically wrong with accountants, he said. Why shouldn't they enjoy the scenery too? I sighed, turned my back on the pear tree and looked out towards the Corinthian Gulf.

A peculiarity of the plain was that our village and the valley were invisible from there; one looked directly out to the sea and the snowy mountains on the opposite shore. It gave the view an immediacy and, to my mind, a nobility; I could imagine a giant taking a mighty step over the water, from mountaintop to mountaintop. That morning Parnassus loomed with unusual clarity, so that each time I looked northwards I was taken aback by the apparent nearness of it.

But my gnawing concern about the future of the village had returned: changes were being made that would alter the mountains forever. "I really can't explain how I feel," I said at length. "Some places deserve respect; otherwise they should just be left alone."

Angelo smiled but did not reply. We both looked out at the sacred mountain across the gulf, and the sight, combined with the quietness of the plain, slowly seduced me back towards serenity.

We made our way home in companionable silence. On that snowy morning at least, we had reached our own plain of understanding.

Chapter Nine

The Ambiguous Hero

E GIRA, THE COASTAL town directly below Chrysambela, is an unprepossessing place, filled with the functional cement flats and shops that have been the curse of Greece since the Second World War. Most of the buildings are crowded along a narrow strip between the main road and the sea. The ugliness of its buildings and the lack of a coherent town plan combine to give Egira a look of shabby meanness that its new-found affluence cannot disguise. The mountains mock the place, for even the poor, neglected villages way above the snow line have a pleasing simplicity and dignity that have eluded Egira.

A railway line runs through the town, and opposite the station is a small square with plane trees, a fountain and a kiosk. At one end of the square is a branch office of the Communist Party of Greece (known as the KKE); not many people visit it nowadays. The little office might well have closed were it not for a local poultry farmer, Christos Menzelopoulos, the man whom Apostoli had described as a hero. Christos opens up the place when he can – makes phone calls, drinks coffee, reads the paper, holds meetings. Young people tend to stay away, he conceded when I talked to him, but he refuses to believe all that stuff about the end of history and the everlasting triumph of capitalism. One day the pendulum would swing back, he said, and the ideals to which he had dedicated his life would live again.

I visited Christos in his office one afternoon in early winter, when the square was carpeted with leaves from the plane trees. He was short, stocky and grey-haired; his manner was open and elusive by turns. He was not sure whether he wanted to talk to me, whether he could trust me. Not many people knew his story now, or wanted to know it, and he was unaccustomed to sharing the details of his past with strangers.

I was curious to hear his story. I wanted to know what it meant to be a hero during the anarchy that had reigned throughout the Occupation and the civil war; for years, I had listened to raised voices arguing over who was to blame for the suffering of those times. But the more I learned about Christos, the more enigmatic he became. He was not generally admired in Egira, and the reservations people expressed about his character did not appear to be determined by their political prejudices alone. He was spoken of as a man who had secrets, the assumption being that he therefore had something to conceal.

It was siesta time, and the square was empty. The little office, with its pictures of Che Guevara and Aris Velouchiotis, one of the Communist founders of the Greek People's Liberation Army

(ELAS), was cold and had no heater. Christos had chosen to meet me here but he now suggested that we catch a cab to his house, where the stove was burning. I was cold too, but I didn't want to move. Christos's reluctance to speak was palpable; I was afraid that he was stalling. And so we sat in that comfortless place as he recounted the events that had overturned his world.

Christos began formally, as though reciting a history lesson, and referred to himself in the third person. But slowly, the rhythm of his narration helped loosen his tongue. Eventually he let forth such a torrent of words that he did not know how to stop them. Each episode he recounted had its own sub-plot, its own chain of complexity; four hours later he had still not done with the telling. In the course of the afternoon he told me, among other things, that he had learned how to tell a story when he was a prisoner on the island of Kefallonia, awaiting execution. He survived that ordeal, in part, because of a secret school that the Communists ran for imprisoned party members. Christos, who came from a poor family, had only attended a village primary school; the Communists taught him how to speak and how to think on his feet. In more ways than one, he would have no story to tell without them.

Christos became involved with the Communists when he joined the National Liberation Front, or EAM, in April 1943, two years after the first German troops entered Athens. Although EAM had been formed by the Communist Party, it cast a wide net. It emphasised practical opposition to the German-controlled government in Athens, rather than ideology; along with its armed wing, ELAS, it soon became the most popular and effective Resistance organisation of the war. Since the German invasion, tens of thousands had died of famine in Athens and Piraeus alone.* Prolonged suffering radicalised the people: they joined

EAM/ELAS in order to oppose the Italians and the Germans, or for humanitarian purposes such as distributing food to the needy. Throughout Greece, thousands of young men like Christos were inspired to 'go to the mountains' to fight for their country's liberty.

Christos decided to join EAM at the suggestion of his friend Yanni, who was also from Versova. During the Occupation, the two men were comrades, but later Yanni moved to the Right and distanced himself from Christos; afterwards, Christos wondered whether Yanni had been suspect from the start. Yanni's neighbour in the village had been a retired general who had served under the dictator Metaxas; had he suggested to Yanni that he join EAM as a spy? Speculations of this kind – suspicions which could never be proved or laid to rest – were just one of the many poisonous consequences of the war and its aftermath.

Christos was a twenty-four-year-old farmer when he joined EAM. His wife, Georgia, was pregnant at the time, with another child underfoot. She had no idea what Christos meant when he announced he was 'going to the mountains'. But theirs was a patriarchal household; Georgia was forced to accept her husband's decision.

The couple had already survived what Georgia believed was the great adventure of her life: they had fallen in love and eloped. It was an act of rebellion that Georgia's parents never forgave; she had been born into a relatively wealthy family and her parents had not wanted her to marry a poor man. The couple survived by working as field hands. During the long years when Christos was with the Resistance and in prison, Georgia's parents refused to give their daughter money, food or even paid work.

In late 1943, Christos left the mountains to work for EAM in Egira, a dangerous undertaking because the Germans were based on the coast. He was given a pistol and a hand grenade for protection; he hid them in a currant stall near the railway line so that he could walk around unarmed. His task was to organise Resistance activities and to monitor troop movements; he also gathered information about local bridges so that explosives experts could work out how best to destroy them.

The German soldiers infected Egira with an ever-present sense of menace. They were instructed to regard all civilians as potential enemies – the occupying army's brutal response to the uncertainties of guerrilla warfare – and were told it was better to shoot once too often than once too seldom. Christos's work in Egira coincided with one of the bloodiest episodes of the war in Greece, which took place in the nearby mountain town of Kalavryta. Guerrillas in the region had abducted and killed seventy-eight soldiers; in retaliation, the Germans burned twenty-five villages around Kalavryta and shot 696 Greeks, including Kalavryta's entire male population.

For Christos, the task of defining the enemy became increasingly complicated. Who was more dangerous: the German soldier or the Greek suspected of collaborating with him? The old social and political certainties had collapsed and he found himself in unmapped territory: a strange, new land of fear, where familiar protocols did not apply.

Dealing with perceived traitors became his most difficult task. How, for example, was Christos to judge a family whose hunger and desperation had led them to co-operate with the enemy? His orders were uncompromising: the traitors' house was to be burned and they were to be marched to the mountains, where they would probably be executed. The family beseeched him to save their skins; the mother wept, clasped his hands and begged for mercy. Did her eight year old son deserve to die? Should her teenage daughter lose her life because of her liaison with an Italian officer? She did not have to plead for long. Christos eventually persuaded his superiors to grant the family a reprieve, although he was not able to prevent their neighbours from ransacking their house.

Such complexities bedevilled his days. The conflict between his instinctive moral response and the uncompromising party line was a recurrent theme in his story. It wound through the events of his life like a tangled thread he was unable to unravel, and eventually became a determining factor in his own fate.

Christos had to juggle the rigid orders of his superiors in the high country with the frailties and compromises he observed on the coast. The Germans were trained to avoid personal contact with the Greeks; they understood that it was easier to kill if the link of common humanity was not recognised. But for Christos the perceived traitors he had to deal with were his neighbours, his own people. In theory, he saw his work as a heroic struggle for liberty, comparable to the struggle for Greek independence against Turkish rule; in practice, however, he was drawn into the shadowland of hatred and envy that continually lurked on the periphery of village life and which the war had thrown into sharp relief.

The execution of the four Philopoulos brothers was a painful example of this process. The family was envied in Arfara for their wealth and disliked for their arrogance; they owned a big flock of sheep and allowed them to wander unchecked over their neighbours' fields. It was said that the brothers were wild and heedless, that they recognised no law but their own. When a neighbour complained to one of the younger boys about the behaviour of the family's sheep, the neighbour was knifed and the crime went unpunished.

The villagers took the matter into their own hands. A document was composed outlining the Philopoulos family's alleged crimes, signed by all the villagers and despatched to the *andartes*. Christos recalled that the document fell short of accusing the boys of co-operating with the Germans; it described them as 'dangerous, bad people'. His superiors ordered him to capture the brothers and take them to the guerrilla camp in the high country.

A night was set aside for the arrest. As Christos and a small band of sympathisers from Versova approached the house, they heard chatter and the clatter of cutlery; the Philopoulos family was celebrating their daughter's engagement. Many guests had been invited; Christos suspected that there were German and Italian soldiers among those enjoying the warmth and good food inside the house. But peeping through the window, he saw that the intended groom was a member of the Communist Party.

Outside, shrouded by the cold night air, the men waited silently and listened as one of the brothers began to play the lute. The music stirred a longing among the waiting men for happier, more peaceful times; times that had somehow become unimaginably distant. As the guests laughed and clapped in appreciation, the hard fact that they were about to send four young men to their deaths impressed itself upon Christos and his helpers.

Christos agonised over how he could carry out his instructions while also saving the boys' lives. He could think of no easy or safe solution. If he let the boys escape, there was the possibility that they would run to the Germans, name members of the Resistance and trigger a chain of slaughter; after all, they would have nothing to lose – such a betrayal would be a logical means of saving their own skins. On the other hand, if Christos abandoned his mission he risked becoming a target of retribution himself.

The men waited until the visitors had left and then swiftly arrested the boys. Christos decided not to take the brothers directly to the *andartes* but to post them in Versova for the night, where they would be safe. It was merely a stalling tactic and in the end it served no purpose. The next day when the brothers were brought before the *andartes*, the Resistance fighters offered to set one of the boys free as a compromise. It was an impossible offer and the brothers refused it, saying "Either all of us are freed, or we die together." And so all four young men perished. Christos was their age, and had grown up in the neighbouring village. He knew that the brothers, at worst, were bullies; even their enemies had not accused them of being traitors. Envy and malice had killed them.

I exclaimed out loud at the injustice of the brothers' death. Christos said that at the time he'd had the same reaction. Years later, however, he decided that his youthful qualms were misjudged. He came to believe that such executions had been necessary in order to prevent further bloodshed; it had been wrong of him to doubt the wisdom of his superiors. The Germans came up to the village on the day of the executions. Who knows what havoc the brothers might have wrought, urged by their own fears and their desire for revenge against the villagers who had betrayed them to the Resistance?

There was a grim postscript to the Philopoulos case. After the execution, one of their neighbours asked Christos if his name had appeared on the document. When Christos said yes, the man blanched: "But I refused to sign." His signature had been forged by his fellow villagers.

The Germans finally fled Greece in late 1944, but the fighting was not yet over: rather than being celebrated as heroes, the *andartes* were condemned as traitors by the monarchists and their British supporters. Athens was fired on by the RAF and British units were involved in fighting in the city, the only occasion during the war when the British turned against Resistance fighters. Churchill was contemptuously dismissive of the *andartes*, describing them as Bolsheviks, or those 'miserable banditti'. He was convinced – mistakenly as it transpired – that British force was necessary to prevent the Communists from controlling Greece. The conflict, a precursor to later Cold War paranoia, represented a bitter reversal for the *andartes* and the beginning of the civil war.

On 24 February 1945 – a cold day, with forty centimetres of snow lying on the ground – the Versova arrests began. Christos had returned to the village; Georgia now suggested that he leave for Athens. But money was necessary for that, and whatever cash the family had made from their small currant crop was needed to live on. Christos, who was recovering from malaria, decided to stay put; in all likelihood, he reasoned, nothing would happen to him.

Since the end of the Occupation, many men who had been Communists or Leftist sympathisers had gone over to the Right, changing their allegiances to save themselves; Christos's old friend Yanni had not been the only villager to switch sides. One such man – let us call him Taki – banged on Christos's door that snowy evening, while Georgia was washing her long, dark hair. During the Occupation, Taki had been a member of the Communist Party; now he was on the doorstep threatening Christos with the same .38 pistol that the party had given him. Behind him were other men from Versova, men whom Christos had known all his life.

Christos and another Communist – the brother of the village school teacher – were marched to the village square, their hands tied with barbed wire. Confusion reigned in the square. Some of Christos's friends were ringing the church bells; the familiar clanging triggered a panic in the arresting party, who feared it was a signal for other *andartes* to come to the prisoners' aid. It was decided to march them on to Egira straightaway.

An old man named Pericles was put in charge of Christos. Pericles had lost two sons during the war. One had been branded a collaborator by the *andartes*, who had executed him; the other, the beloved younger son, had been killed by the Germans. As Pericles marched him down the road to Egira, Christos spoke to him of the younger boy. He reminded Pericles that the *andartes* had avenged his son's death, which was their way of seeking justice. Christos's urgently whispered words made the old man weep. "You are right to remind me of this," he said. "I promise not to harm you."

In a village near the coast a third man was arrested, and he and Christos were tied together. The three prisoners were dragged through the muddy swamps that then surrounded Egira, and eventually imprisoned in a house near the sea, along with other members of the Resistance. Christos, who was still weak from his bout of malaria, was periodically beaten and doused in cold water. His tormentors were locals; he recognised a police-man and a baker. One prisoner, who was beaten repeatedly on the soles of his feet, had a knife and wanted to take his revenge, but Christos warned him not to: "If you do, they'll kill us all."

After three days and nights the prisoners were tied together and marched to Egio. Along the way they passed a truckload of *andartes*. But the guerrillas were powerless to help their former comrades: they had recently given up their weapons as part of the Varkiza agreement, in which they had agreed to disarm in return for an amnesty for 'political' crimes, a plebiscite on the monarchy and general elections. The treaty was never honoured.

When the prisoners finally arrived in Egio, they were jeered by a crowd. "Traitors!" "Bulgarians!" Along with three other men who had worked with him in the Resistance, Christos was charged with executing six people in one day. It was alleged that they had used a knife and the jagged edge of a tin can, using the can itself as a container for the eyes they gouged from the dead.

The trial took place in Messolongi, the town where Lord Byron had died of malaria during the Greek War of Independence. Messolongi was on the other side of the Corinthian Gulf, a region where Christos was a stranger; people whom he did not know testified against him. The evidence was flimsy to say the least; the prosecutor himself did not believe that there was enough to convict the accused for murder. But the jury – swayed perhaps by the prejudices of their foreman, who was an influential lawyer in the region, or the brutality of the charges, or even by their own experiences of the war – sentenced the four men to death.

While awaiting execution, Christos was to be jailed on the island of Kefallonia in the Ionian Sea. He was not the only Communist prisoner on Kefallonia to be accused of fabricated crimes, but many of his fellow Leftists had resigned themselves to death; they had lost faith in their ability to save themselves. Years of fighting and deprivation had worn them down. Perhaps the blackening of the Resistance movement and the rise of the despised collaborators had broken their spirits, or maybe they were sickened by what they had witnessed, or by what they had done.

For Christos, however, the matter was straightforward: he was innocent and deserved to live. Alone in his cell, his thoughts circled obsessively around the coil of lies in which he had been trapped. The charges maligned his character and his beloved cause. He had been prepared to give his life for his country; he would not lose it now because of a falsehood. A slender hope began to take hold. He had assumed that the names of his so-called victims were fictitious. But what if they referred to real people? What if his 'victims' were alive and could be found? The prison held about twenty-five men who, like him, were from the Achaïa district of the northern Peloponnese. The mountain villages were tribal, closed communities; if his so-called victims really existed, there was a chance that one of the prisoners would know them.

In the early days of his incarceration, the prisoners were not allowed to have contact with each other, but, like his fellow inmates, Christos saw the cook every day. He gave him the names of the six people he was accused of murdering and asked him to question his compatriots about them. The next evening, the cook came back with good news: two of the victims – a woman called Tasia and a man called Dimitri – were known to be living in mountain villages above Egio. Another prisoner later identified a third man on the list: a fellow called Spiros, who was serving as a police officer in Macedonia. The prisoner suggested that Christos contact Spiros's father, who lived in the mountains above Patras.

The next step was to find these people. Georgia would have to do this, and it would mean travelling by foot over the mountains, with the civil war still raging; the *andartes* had threatened to kill people who left their villages during that dangerous time. Georgia did not hesitate.

In asking his wife to risk her life for him, Christos told her a lie. He said that if the three alleged victims were found alive, he would be out of jail within six months. This was necessary, he said, to give her courage.

><<

I was introduced to Georgia on my second meeting with Christos, which took place in their house on a hill above Egira. We sat together in their modest kitchen, warmed by their wood-fired stove. She was softly spoken and gentle, as Christos had described, and she grasped my hand in both of hers as though I were a long lost friend. She told me that in the lean years when Christos was away working for the Resistance, my grandmother Katerina had sometimes left loaves of bread on her doorstep; she would not knock and always crept away before Georgia could thank her. Tears came into Georgia's eyes and she stroked my cheek with her finger. "You look like her," she said.

Georgia's voice rarely rose above a whisper. She sat close to me, her hands in her lap, a barely suppressed smile hovering around her lips and eyes. Over the years, my respect for women such as Georgia had deepened. It seemed to me that years of hardship had left them with a knack for the expressive, unself-conscious gesture; with a deft word or look they drew the invisible threads of the world around them. I thought of Varvara, another woman from the village, whose husband had died the previous winter. When I expressed sympathy for her loss, she automatically clasped my hand, smiled and walked away; she had forgotten who I was. Ten days later, I met her again. Drawing me to her, she kissed me on the forehead and patted my hair as though in blessing. "I love you," she said.

I wanted to hear more of Georgia's story, but Christos was the one who was accustomed to speaking; he told me gruffly to leave his wife alone. "Why do you want to know these bad things? She hid so they would not find her, she caught an infection, she was tyrannised. Georgia's tears have watered the hills." Christos knew that his decision to join EAM had been the main cause of Georgia's suffering and he still did not like to be reminded of it. Georgia herself dismissed my questions with a shrug: "The point is that all I went through cannot be written in one story. It doesn't end, not even if you talk all day."

So Georgia did not tell me much about how she came to find the people Christos was supposed to have murdered. But her deeds spoke for themselves. First, she had to face a bureaucratic battle: each time she wanted to leave the village to help Christos, she became enmeshed in the arduous rigmarole of obtaining travel documents. Then there was the much greater ordeal of walking to the mountain villages along stony tracks, at a time when, in Christos's words, travelling strangers were "killed like birds." And finally, Georgia had to convince her quarries to give evidence on behalf of her husband, a despised Communist.

The only one of the three who readily agreed to help her was the father of Spiros, the policeman stationed in Macedonia, whom Georgia found in a mountain village above Patras. As she walked through this steep and unfamiliar country, her shoes pinched her feet and she lost the heel on one of them. So she continued barefooted along the stony track. When she finally arrived in the village she saw a priest. Georgia was, and continues to be, a devout woman. She asked the priest where she could find the man she wanted but he told her that no such person existed. Luckily, a neighbour overheard them and told Georgia that the man she sought lived just ten metres away. When

Georgia finally found him she began to weep with exhaustion and relief. "Stop crying, please, my dear," he said. "My son lives. I am willing to help you."

It took Christos's lawyer two years to persuade the courts to hear the new evidence, by which time five of the six people on the list of 'victims' had been found. But even so, Christos was not released until 1957, after being imprisoned for twelve years.

><

The civil war ostensibly divided Greece into two sides, the Left and the Right, but the reality was far more complex. During the war some Leftists were conscripted by the national army and forced to fight their former comrades, while some members of the Resistance, as we have seen, willingly changed allegiances and betrayed men they had fought beside. While telling his story, Christos freely acknowledged those occasions when he had been helped by a stranger or a political opponent: the fair-minded prosecutor at his trial; the old man whose son Christos had supposedly killed; the establishment figures who eventually responded to his lawyer's pleas to reverse his sentence. Such times, when family ties or the bond of friendship or the spontaneous outpouring of sympathy overrode political divisions, were an important part of his narrative and integral to his understanding of human nature.

And yet, paradoxically, Christos carried his awareness of the importance of the personal response side by side with his loyalty to the Communist Party. The contradiction might explain the following story and also why he was reluctant to tell it; fifty years on, Christos did not want to damage the cause for which he had sacrificed so much.

In 1944, towards the end of the Occupation, Christos was asked to move prisoners held by the *andartes* in the mountains above Egio. He was to take them to a higher, more inaccessible place, as the Germans were advancing. The camp held 186 people – 148 men and thirty-eight women. Many of the men were wealthy landowners, business people and citizens suspected of collaborating with the Germans or of being sympathetic to the Right, while many of the women were prostitutes.

Christos felt that some of the prisoners were not really traitors at all. "Those women they accused of having sexual relations with the Germans, for instance. Had they got into that with the intention of betraying their country or because they were hungry? I just wanted to get to the truth and I had to decide what that was . . ."

Ten armed men helped Christos to move the prisoners. Along the march they passed a river, and Christos decided that this would be a good place to stop and rest. Many of the women were weak, as they were suffering from venereal disease; the men too were tired and thirsty.

The *andartes* helping Christos took him to task. "Maybe because they looked upon these people as traitors, my comrades did not want me to be kind to the prisoners."

But Christos believed that a Communist should look at the situation with a humanitarian eye. "What is a Communist?" he said to me. "Someone who is prepared to sacrifice their life for the common good. How should I regard you? As someone whom I should protect. How should I do this? With my life. Why else would I give it?

"And so there we were. We were arguing among ourselves, we were all armed, and the prisoners heard the fuss and thought they were about to be executed."

The prisoners understood that Christos was defending them, but they believed he did much more than defend their right to rest by a river: they believed that his intervention saved their lives, that they had been taken to the river for a mass execution.

I had first heard this story from the son of one of the prisoners, Kosta Dimopoulos. His father, Efthimios, a wealthy landowner from Egio, had no doubt whatsoever that Christos had saved his life by disobeying orders that day and setting his prisoners free. Apostoli once told me about a chance meeting he'd witnessed between Efthimios and Christos, more than forty years after the war. Efthimios was overcome by emotion when he saw the old Communist; he embraced him tearfully and with humility, kissed his hands and called him his "saviour."

But Christos became impatient when I mentioned this story and insisted that Efthimios was mistaken. I later told Kosta that Christos had denied saving his father's life. The denial irritated Kosta; he could make no sense of it. Christos and his father were not friends, they did not socialise and their political beliefs were incompatible; yet when Efthimios died, Christos had been disappointed that he had not been informed. He had wanted to attend the funeral, a sign that he felt a significant connection with Efthimios.

Georgia, likewise, believed that Christos saved the prisoners that day. "Don't listen to him," she whispered to me after Christos had related his version of the events. "He saved the lives of all those people."

But Christos had long refused any public credit for the deed, declining to speak of it even during his trial, when his life was at stake. An influential businessman, one of the prisoners whom Christos was said to have saved, offered to testify on his behalf and Georgia urged her husband to accept. But Christos did not take up the offer. The man's testimony would have been false, he said, and besides, it would have meant saving his own skin by accusing those higher up in the party of brutality. And so he remained silent. By refusing to take credit for an independent act of kindness, Christos not only kept faith with his cause but also with his own sense that he was part of a greater historical movement. Without that belief, his experiences during the war were in danger, perhaps, of being cast not as a heroic struggle, but as a series of bloody and brutal events.

"What is a Communist? Someone who is prepared to sacrifice their life for the common good. How should I regard you? As someone whom I should protect. How should I do this? With my life . . ."

* The exact number of people who died because of the famine is not known. In *Inside Hitler's Greece*, historian Mark Mazower argues that official statistics from the period tend to underestimate the actual rate of mortality, since many deaths were not announced to the authorities, and that hunger contributed to deaths from other causes, such as tuberculosis and influenza. Mazower estimates that famine 'probably caused more than 40,000 deaths' in Athens and Piraeus in the winter of 1941.

Endings

DESPITE THE TIMID protestations of his wife, Apostoli began to harvest his olives on a Tuesday, an ill-omened day in the Greek world ever since the Tuesday when Constantinople fell to the Turks. Apostoli was unwilling to delay the single biggest task of his year; the olives were ready and the deep winter cold had not yet set in. He was determined to proceed.

As the harvest approached, the village became more and more preoccupied with the problem of who would pick the fruit. Each year it became increasingly difficult for the elderly householders to look after their inheritance. Old widow Pinio, for instance, had given up the struggle. Her son in Athens had no interest in the family land and she was too frail to do the work alone, so her fields were covered with brambles and her olives rotted on the ground. Once the great tin drums in her kitchen had been filled to the brim with virgin oil; now they were empty and she bought the stuff by the litre from her neighbours.

Pinio's predicament was a warning to the other villagers, who did what they could to stave off the inevitable. Since 1991, Albanian workers had provided a partial solution, but because most of them entered the country illegally they were vulnerable to deportation. During the olive season, when itinerant Albanians walked up to the villages to secure work and lodgings, the police followed close behind. Although the number of foreign workers far outstripped the number of arrests, most of the Albanians preferred to keep on the move. As a consequence, many village families had no reliable way of securing workers from season to season. They did not know when – or if – their labourers would return until the harvest was upon them.

When the Albanians first came to the village, they were regarded with hostility and suspicion. It takes a great deal of stamina, however, to maintain a contemptuous distance from a man who works beside you all day and who shares your bread at night. The illegal immigrants were generally paid half as much as Greek workers, but because they had no home of their own, full board was often part of the deal. Most of the villagers eventually came to pity these men who were so starved that they would eat an entire loaf with each meal, day after day. Workers who were once expected to bed down in the barn at night were gradually invited to sleep inside the house. My cousin Nick converted his barn into a small dormitory for the Albanians, complete with a gas jet, a little pot for making coffee and a wood-fired heater. Vassiliki's workers slept in her spare room, and ate with her and her husband at night as a matter of course.

Apostoli too was dependent on outside help. His father's bequest had to be maintained, and he was the only worker left in the family; Katina was recovering from an operation and was not fit for the fields any more, and while Peter was young and strong, he was busy teaching in Akrata.

My grandfather, Vassili, had worked well into his eighties. In his youth he had planted as many olive trees as he could; at one time he had been the biggest land-holder in Versova. Apostoli had spent many years chafing at his father's conscientious example before finally accepting that the work was his life too; now he neither knew nor desired any other.

Apostoli's large holdings were immaculately maintained; the sorry business of waiting for workers who might not show up was something that he was not prepared to tolerate. His solution was to hire Zissi and Diamanti, a husband and wife of Greek descent who had fled their ancestral home in Albania. They had been born on the fertile coast that overlooks Corfu and still owned land there. Zissi had been an electrician in a Government smallgoods factory, while Diamanti had taught Greek as a second language; when Communism collapsed, the couple lost their jobs. Because of their heritage they were granted legal residency in Greece, but the nature of loyalty and patriotism is tricky; its wells run deep. In Albania, the family had lived in a Greek milieu, but Greece itself, with its shops and traffic, its television and electronic music, struck them as a greedy, undisciplined and alarming place.

Zissi and Diamanti's misfortune was Apostoli's opportunity. He found the couple industrious and capable, and so paid them a full Greek wage. It was almost impossible to find Greek agricultural workers of any kind, let alone workers of this quality; Zissi and Diamanti were his 'saviours'. One summer he had travelled to Albania with them and visited their home. The sight of their deserted fields and the senseless destruction of buildings, trees and vines that had taken place in the region during the Hoxha regime's dying days had disturbed and saddened him. "If only you knew how I pitied them."

Once the olive season had begun, Angelo and I would often walk to the fields to join Apostoli and his workers. Most of the villagers set out for the fields before dawn, but we were not so conscientious. After breakfast, we walked through Versova's near-deserted streets, past stone houses whose shutters were still closed because the owners had left in the dark. The road we took wound into the valley at the bottom of the village, where cherry trees and newly planted vineyards waited for the cold weather to pass. As the road dipped, the olives took over and we saw our neighbours bustling among the treetops. They would wave and shout out greetings: How much did we charge for a day's labour? Were we just tourists after all? One day, our friend Yiota called out to us as she spread a tarpaulin under a tree to catch the fruit. Her husband had fallen ill and she had to manage with only one Albanian labourer, although she had hoped for two. The Albanian was young, inexperienced and spoke no Greek; he looked clumsy and uncertain as he leaned forward from his perch to comb the olive branches. Yiota knew she could not expect him to prune the trees – he did not have the necessary skills – and she was not strong enough to do it herself.

Apostoli scowled when we told him about Yiota's dilemma. He liked her, but he was in no position to help. And her bad luck would affect her harvest for the following season. "When you fertilise a tree you are merely pleading with it to bear fruit," he explained. "When you prune, you are ordering it to."

Zissi and Diamanti had once tended olives and vines of their own; they needed neither supervision nor instruction. It was pleasant to work beside them in the winter sunshine, as they deftly knocked the olives from the trees with sticks in the Albanian style. If their circumstances caused them any bitterness, they kept it to themselves. "Tell your brother to rest a little," said Zissi to Angelo after we had been gathering olives for a while. "We are here now and there is no need for him to work so hard."

Apostoli did what he could to keep pace with his workers, but his face was drawn and pale by the end of the day. Once he was home he would sit for an hour or two, smoking and staring into the fire. His unstated anxieties about the difficulty of the work, and the question of how long he would be able to continue it, crept over the house for the duration of the season. He lightened up during his visits to the olive-oil factory on the edge of the village, when he would stand and watch as the clanking machinery transformed his crop into a shiny, green stream. Gypsy boys would gather around, greedily placing slices of stale bread under the fresh oil as it poured into a vat. "It's the best in Greece you know," Apostoli would tell them with quiet gravity, as though the boys were connoisseurs in disguise. "It's the very best in Greece."

Katina shared her husband's pride in the oil, but harvest time made her uneasy too. The job of providing a cooked midday meal for the workers had been taken over by Peter's wife, Lily. Left alone in the house with no pressing task at hand brought on a mood of agitated melancholy in Katina; she would remember all the years she'd worked in the fields, for no thanks and no pay, beside men who expected her to put in a full day and also prepare their supper at the end of it.

During the harvest only school children and old ladies were

left in the village. It filled up again at dusk when the workers would gather, talking lazily and drinking coffee on doorsteps. The Albanians were mostly skinny and young; when I walked past them they would blow smoke rings and swagger a little. Angelo said they reminded him of himself during his early years in Australia.

Although the villagers had come to rely on them, the labourers did not solve the problem of who would inherit the fertile fields and olive groves when the old folk passed on. Agricultural labour had become the domain of the poor. In the end, it was prosperity that was killing the village: wealth had bred indifference to the land that had made it possible.

Because my feelings on the subject ran high, I had refrained from asking what the fate of my family's land would be. Vassili had divided his holdings between his five children on the understanding that whoever worked a particular field would earn the profit from it. So the small olive grove that belonged to Angelo, and which would one day belong to me, was tended by Apostoli and his workers. It was on a site called Kakodiava – or bad road – because of the muddy track that had once led to it. The olives grew on a terrace with views of Evrestina. I liked the place but had to be walked through the maze of tracks and trees that surrounded it; I could not find it by myself. Unless we moved to Greece I knew it was unlikely that I would have a say in the olive grove's future. Yet I would not be able to disguise my disappointment if the land was ever given up. I knew that that decision rightly belonged to the people who lived in the village; I did not believe that Apostoli, Katina and their children should be made to feel responsible for whatever meaning the land may have held for me. But all the same, I found myself hoping that my son would inherit the land one day and that he would also enjoy the simple pleasure of knocking the fruit from the trees and take pride in the heavy, full-flavoured oil that grew from its stony soil.

Sometimes, the words we keep to ourselves are communicated despite our best intentions. On a still winter morning, just days before I was due to leave for Australia, my cousin Peter told me not to worry about the future of Angelo's olive grove. He said he was prepared to take over all of our family's land when Apostoli could no longer manage.

"All our lives are here," said Peter simply. "This is who we are." He had hung back from helping Apostoli, not only because of his teaching work, but because he believed it was the most tactful course. The olive groves, the currant vines, the cherry orchards and the vineyards: this was his father's domain. For six decades they had determined when Apostoli ate and when he slept, how he worked and for how long he rested. And that was how it would remain, Peter said, until the season came when his father decided otherwise.

>◄

During the fourteen weeks that I had been in Greece, I had hardly thought of home. I have always been this way: I travel without homesickness, a fact of which I have always felt slightly ashamed. And yet I knew that when I did return to Australia, I would be glad to see family, friends and familiar places once more, and that what I had made of my life would fill me up again.

When in Australia I was a poor correspondent. Writing in Greek was not easy and I did not like to be confronted with the gulf that lay between my Greek and Australian worlds. Occasionally I'd wake feeling anxious and guilty because I had not contacted the people whom I loved in Greece. I was afraid that my family or my neighbours in the village would have forgotten me; that I would be punished somehow for leaving them so long.

And yet when I did go back, I found that I was able to move into their lives once more, to quietly pick up the threads that connected us. I was allowed, again and again, to step over the line and to slip back into Greek time, as though into an unawakened part of my own self. And more than this, I was rewarded for my divided loyalties with more love than I knew how to return.

In the last few days I had spent in the village, I had realised that, had my circumstances been different, I would have been prepared to stay on. In the past, my lack of ease with Greek had eventually propelled me back to Australia. Reading, writing and talking was how I got by, how I earned my keep; living in Greece would mean giving up the domain that felt most natural to me. On this journey my relationship with Greek had continued to be idiosyncratic and unpredictable: sometimes I was able to unlock my tongue and speak without self-consciousness, at other times my words came out in an embarrassed, syntactically confused stammer. Witticisms were impossible, small talk was painful; I only spoke when it was necessary. But gradually I had come to regard my lack of fluency as a paradoxical gift: it had helped me understand that it was not words that bound me to these people, after all.

><

About three months after I came back to Australia, Apostoli paid us a surprise visit. It was the longest trip he had ever made and he himself was astonished by it. But after a week, or maybe even less, it was clear to us all that he wanted to go home. The streets in Melbourne were so flat and still and the people were so reserved and there was no *kafeneion* to visit at night. He couldn't understand what the good citizens did all day and why they seemed to spend so much time alone.

I asked him what news he had of the village and he said that old Chryssoula, his neighbour, had finally died. "I don't know what she did to deserve such a death, what kind of a curse had been put on her," he said. "But she was neglected and had sores on her body when she went. Her death went on for a long time."

He said that on the day of Chryssoula's death, his daughter Kostandina had visited Chrysambela. Kostandina lived in Egio with her husband and her daughter. She was the one in the family who was said to have inherited Grandmother Katerina's great kindness of heart. She went directly to Chryssoula's bed. When she saw the old lady in all her wretchedness, she took her face in her hands and began to kiss her, saying: "Oh my love, my dear one, how sad it makes me to see you this way."

The old lady died soon after Kostandina left the room, having at last received the tenderness she had been waiting for.

LONELY PLANET JOURNEYS

JOURNEYS is a unique collection of travel writing – published by the company that understands travel better than anyone else.

It is a series for anyone who has ever experienced – or dreamed of – the magical moment when they encountered a strange culture or saw a place for the first time. They are tales to read while you're planning a trip, while you're on the road or while you're in an armchair, in front of a fire.

These outstanding titles explore our planet through the eyes of a diverse group of international writers. JOURNEYS books catch the spirit of a place, illuminate a culture, recount an adventure, or introduce a fascinating way of life. They always entertain, and always enrich the experience of travel.

'Lively, intelligent and varied . . . an important contribution to travel literature' – *Melbourne Age*

FULL CIRCLE
A South American Journey
Luis Sepúlveda (translated by Chris Andrews)

'A journey without a fixed itinerary' in the company of Chilean writer Luis Sepúlveda. Extravagant characters and extraordinary situations are memorably evoked: gauchos organising a tournament of lies, a scheming heiress on the lookout for a husband, a pilot with a corpse on board his plane . . . Part autobiography, part travel memoir, *Full Circle* brings us the distinctive voice of one of South America's most compelling writers.

WINNER 1996 Astrolabe – Etonnants Voyageurs award for the best work of travel literature published in France.

THE GATES OF DAMASCUS
Lieve Joris (translated by Sam Garrett)

This best-selling book is a beautifully drawn portrait of day-to-day life in modern Syria. Through her intimate contact with local people, Lieve Joris draws us into the fascinating world that lies behind the gates of Damascus. Hala's husband is a political prisoner, jailed for his opposition to the Assad regime; through the author's friendship with Hala we see how Syrian politics impacts on the lives of ordinary people.

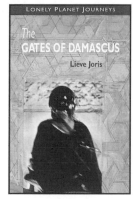

Written after the Gulf War, *The Gates of Damascus* offers a unique insight into the complexities of the Arab world.

IN RAJASTHAN
Royina Grewal

As she writes of her travels through Rajasthan, Indian writer Royina Grewal takes us behind the exotic facade of this fabled destination: here is an insider's perceptive account of India's most colourful state. *In Rajasthan* discusses folk music and architecture, feudal traditions and regional cuisine . . . Most of all, it focuses on people – from maharajas to camel trainers, from politicians to itinerant snake charmers – to convey the excitement and challenges of a region in transition.

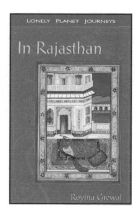

ISLANDS IN THE CLOUDS
Travels in the Highlands of New Guinea
Isabella Tree

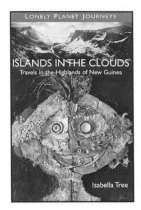

This is the fascinating account of a journey to the remote and beautiful Highlands of Papua New Guinea and Irian Jaya: one of the most extraordinary and dangerous regions on the planet. The author travels with a PNG Highlander who introduces her to his intriguing and complex world, which is changing rapidly as it collides with twentieth-century technology and the island's developing social and political systems. *Islands in the Clouds* is a thoughtful, moving book, full of insights into a region that is rarely noticed by the rest of the world.

KINGDOM OF THE FILM STARS
Journey into Jordan
Annie Caulfield

Kingdom of the Film Stars is a travel book and a love story. With honesty and humour, Annie Caulfield writes of travelling in Jordan and falling in love with a Bedouin with film-star looks.

The author offers fascinating insights into the country – from the tent life of traditional women to the hustle of downtown Amman. *Kingdom of the Film Stars* unpicks tight-woven Western myths about the Arab world, presenting cultural and political issues within the intimate framework of a compelling love story.

LOST JAPAN
Alex Kerr

Lost Japan draws on the author's personal experiences of Japan over thirty years. Alex Kerr takes his readers on a backstage tour, exploring different facets of his involvement with the country: friendships with Kabuki actors, buying and selling art, studying calligraphy, exploring rarely visited temples and shrines . . .

The Japanese edition of this book was awarded the 1994 Shincho Gakugei Literature Prize for the best work of non-fiction: the first time a foreigner has won this prestigious award.

THE RAINBIRD
A Central African Journey
Jan Brokken
(translated by Sam Garrett)

The Rainbird is a classic travel story. Following in the footsteps of famous Europeans such as Albert Schweitzer and H.M. Stanley, Jan Brokken journeyed to Gabon in central Africa. A kaleidoscope of adventures and anecdotes, *The Rainbird* brilliantly chronicles the encounter between Africa and Europe as it was acted out on a side-street of history. It is also the compelling, immensely readable account of the author's own travels in one of the most remote and mysterious regions of Africa.

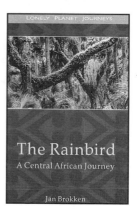

SEAN & DAVID'S LONG DRIVE

Sean Condon

Sean and David are young townies who have rarely strayed beyond city limits. One day, for no good reason, they set out to discover their homeland, and what follows is a wildly entertaining adventure that covers half of Australia. Highlights include the weekly Hair Wax Report and a Croc-Spotting with Stew adventure.

Sean Condon has written a hilarious, offbeat road book that mixes sharp insights with deadpan humour and outright lies.

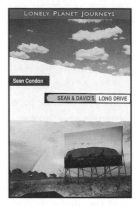

SHOPPING FOR BUDDHAS

Jeff Greenwald

Here in this distant, exotic land, we were compelled to raise the art of shopping to an experience that was, on the one hand, almost Zen – and, on the other hand, tinged with desperation like shopping at Macy's or Bloomingdale's during a one-day-only White Sale.

Shopping for Buddhas is Jeff Greenwald's story of his obsessive search for the perfect Buddha statue. In the backstreets of Kathmandu, he discovers more than he bargained for . . . and his souvenir-hunting turns into an ironic metaphor for the clash between spiritual riches and material greed. Politics, religion and serious shopping collide in this witty account of an enlightening visit to Nepal.

WINNER of the Gold Medal for the Best Travel Book, Society of American Travel Writers' Lowell Thomas Journalism Awards.

SONGS TO AN AFRICAN SUNSET
A Zimbabwean Story
Sekai Nzenza-Shand

Songs to an African Sunset braids vividly personal stories into an intimate picture of contemporary Zimbabwe. Returning to her family's village after many years in the West, Sekai Nzenza-Shand discovers a world where ancestor worship, polygamy and witchcraft still govern the rhythms of daily life – and where drought, deforestation and AIDS have wrought devastating changes. With insight and affection, she explores a culture torn between respect for the old ways and the irresistible pull of the new.

RELATED TITLES FROM LONELY PLANET

Greece

With this informative book as your guide you'll discover a country of timeless pleasures, island hideaways, quiet mountain groves and local tavernas. Our guidebook is packed with cultural and historical information and reliable advice for every budget.

Trekking in Greece

Mountainous landscapes, the solitude of ancient pathways and secluded beaches await those who extend their horizons beyond Athens and the antiquities. Covers the main trekking regions and includes contoured maps of trekking routes.

Mediterranean Europe on a shoestring

All the travel advice and essential information you'll need for travel in Albania, Andorra, Bosnia-Hercegovina, Croatia, Cyprus, France, Greece, Italy, Macedonia, Malta, Morocco, Portugal, Slovenia, Spain, Tunisia, Turkey and Yugoslavia.

Western Europe on a shoestring

This practical guide provides concise information for budget travellers heading for Ireland or Greece, Portugal or the Netherlands, and everywhere in between.

Greek phrasebook

Whether you want to catch an inter-island ferry, explore ancient ruins or propose a toast with your retsina, this phrasebook will help you choose the right words for any occasion.

Mediterranean Europe phrasebook

You'll be able to ask for directions to galleries, museums and cafes in Albanian, Greek, Italian, Macedonian, Maltese, Serbian & Croatian and Slovene.

Western Europe phrasebook

Show your appreciation for the great masters in Basque, Catalan, Dutch, French, German, Greek, Irish, Italian, Portuguese, Scottish (Gaelic), Spanish (Castilian) and Welsh.

PLANET TALK

Lonely Planet's FREE quarterly newsletter

Every issue of PLANET TALK is packed with up-to-date travel news and advice including:

- a letter from Lonely Planet founders Tony and Maureen Wheeler
- travel diary from a Lonely Planet author
  – find out what it's really like out on the road
- feature article on an important and topical travel issue
- a selection of recent letters from our readers
- the latest travel news from all over the world
- details on Lonely Planet's new and forthcoming releases

To join our mailing list contact any Lonely Planet office.

LONELY PLANET PUBLICATIONS

Australia: PO Box 617, Hawthorn 3122, Victoria
tel: (03) 9819 1877 fax: (03) 9819 6459
e-mail: talk2us@lonelyplanet.com.au

USA: Embarcadero West, 155 Filbert St, Suite 251,
Oakland, CA 94607
tel: (510) 893 8555 TOLL FREE: 800 275-8555
fax: (510) 893 8563 e-mail: info@lonelyplanet.com

UK: 10 Barley Mow Passage, Chiswick, London W4 4PH
tel: (0181) 742 3161 fax: (0181) 742 2772
e-mail: 100413.3551@compuserve.com

France: 71 bis rue du Cardinal Lemoine, 75005 Paris
tel: 1 44 32 06 20 fax: 1 46 34 72 55
e-mail: 100560.415@compuserve.com

World Wide Web: Lonely Planet is now accesible via the World Wide Web. For travel information and an up-to-date catalogue, you can find us at http://www.lonelyplanet.com/

THE LONELY PLANET STORY

Lonely Planet published its first book in 1973 in response to the numerous 'How did you do it?' questions Maureen and Tony Wheeler were asked after driving, bussing, hitching, sailing and railing their way from England to Australia.

Written at a kitchen table and hand collated, trimmed and stapled, *Across Asia on the Cheap* became an instant local bestseller, inspiring thoughts of another book.

Eighteen months in South-East Asia resulted in their second guide, *South-East Asia on a shoestring*, which they put together in a backstreet Chinese hotel in Singapore in 1975. The 'yellow bible' as it quickly became known to backpackers around the world, soon became *the* guide to the region. It has sold well over half a million copies and is now in its 9th edition, still retaining its familiar yellow cover.

Today there are over 240 titles, including travel guides, walking guides, language kits & phrasebooks, travel atlases and travel literature. The company is the largest independent travel publisher in the world. Although Lonely Planet initially specialised in guides to Asia, today there are few corners of the globe that have not been covered.

The emphasis continues to be on travel for independent travellers. Tony and Maureen still travel for several months of each year and play an active part in the writing, updating and quality control of Lonely Planet's guides.

They have been joined by over 70 authors and 170 staff at our offices in Melbourne (Australia), Oakland (USA), London (UK) and Paris (France). Travellers themselves also make a valuable contribution to the guides through the feedback we receive in thousands of letters each year and on our web site.

The people at Lonely Planet strongly believe that travellers can make a positive contribution to the countries they visit, both through their appreciation of the countries' culture, wildlife and natural features, and through the money they spend. In addition, the company makes a direct contribution to the countries and regions it covers. Since 1986 a percentage of the income from each book has been donated to ventures such as famine relief in Africa; aid projects in India; agricultural projects in Central America; Greenpeace's efforts to halt French nuclear testing in the Pacific; and Amnesty International.

'I hope we send people out with the right attitude about travel. You realise when you travel that there are so many different perspectives about the world, so we hope these books will make people more interested in what they see.'

– Tony Wheeler